MEDIA AND COMMUNICATIONS - TECHNOLOGIES, POLICIES AND CHALLENGES

THE SYMBOL AND THE REASON

AN INTRODUCTION TO PUBLIC RELATIONS

MEDIA AND COMMUNICATIONS - TECHNOLOGIES, POLICIES AND CHALLENGES

Additional books in this series can be found on Nova's website under the Series tab.

Additional e-books in this series can be found on Nova's website under the eBooks tab.

MEDIA AND COMMUNICATIONS -
TECHNOLOGIES, POLICIES AND CHALLENGES

THE SYMBOL AND THE REASON

AN INTRODUCTION TO PUBLIC RELATIONS

LUKE STRONGMAN

NOTICE TO THE READER

Library of Congress Cataloging-in-Publication Data

ISBN: 978-1-53612-487-3

Published by Nova Science Publishers, Inc. † New York

CONTENTS

PREFACE

This book is a critical and practical guide to the aspects of public relations in the everyday business world. It explores key thematical trends and developments within the public relations and reputation management fields. Public Relations is essential to any business or organisational entity; it is a part of what they do in performing their function and it is a part of what helps them to perform their function. Pubic relation is what links organisations' values and products to their stakeholders as well as to the market and social drivers that sustain them. Public relations practitioners are change-merchants. That is, they like to shift public opinion and bring about new attitudes and behaviours. Including chapters that discuss issues such as crisis management, negotiation, networking, and branding, this book delves beneath the surface activity to reveal the theory behind the practice. This will be an accessible, interesting book that will appeal to broaden general readership, including a wide variety of everyday business viewpoints.

ACKNOWLEDGMENTS

Thank you to my publisher, Nova Science, to colleagues at the Open Polytechnic, family and friends. Selected quotations from the esteemed Public Relations practitioners included in the book come from *Brainy Quote.*

Chapter 1

'TWO WAY STREET': PUBLIC RELATIONS IN CONTEXT

'Either write something worth reading or do something worth writing about'
– Benjamin Franklin

'PR', or 'Public Relations' is a branch of communication, marketing and human resources that is broad and multi-disciplinary, and increasingly essential to the business world. As a subject and an organisational practice, it is simultaneously simple and difficult to understand. Sometimes it seems like a mist that touches no one and everyone, sometimes like laser that illuminates issues, people, concepts and organisations in 'supra-reality'. Public Relations is essential to any business or organisational entity, it is a part of what they do in performing their function, and it is a part of what helps them to perform their function. Public Relations is what links organisations' values and products with its stakeholders and with the market and social drivers that sustain them. Public Relations is a dialogue, a 'two way street.' Arising in classical culture in the concept of *Arctūrus* or 'keeper of boundaries', Public Relations concerns an entity's, organisation's or person's market segmentation and *becomes* a part of that audience in 'announcing' itself. It is a reflexive activity. Public Relations is eight-tenths focused on communication and it both constitutes and changes organisational practice. Public Relations practitioners are change-merchants, they like to shift public opinion and bring about new attitudes and behaviours. As Noam Chomsky once stated: '[t]he process of shaping opinion, attitudes, and perceptions was termed the 'engineering of consent' by one of the founders of the modern Public Relations industry, Edward Bernays.' This has spawned the massive popularity of the phrase 'manufacturing consent,' coined by Chomsky himself in a book of the same title [1].

However, 'manufacturing consent' or in fact persuading others is not always an easy task, particularly if the weight of popular opinion has swung against your client -- a group of people believes that X is so, and the organisation you represent, would like them to believe that Y is so. Your client is 'super-professional' but some groups believe he or he is immoral, because of that little kiss in the boardroom photo. How to gain consumer attention, to acquire and maintain mutual lines of communication, understanding, acceptance and co-operation between organisation and its publics, requires constant mediation and reflection. How to stay informed on public opinion, serve the public's interest, define roles, act as an early warning system, and to anticipate trends. and to research and provide ethical advice on the best communication techniques and principle creative tools, takes skill, knowledge, planning ability and an ability to reduce the complex to its smallest substrate. Public Relations must be deliberate, engage with a variety of types and audiences, it must advocate responsibility, and a 'wider duty of care' in organisation or to a group of stakeholders. Based on empathy and understanding, storytelling and creativity, Public Relations uses tools from psychology, business and marketing. At its virtuous best, it involves a mutuality between stakeholders, a duty of care and in an everyday sense an exchange in viewpoints in relationships. As Roberts-Bowman (2016) argues, Public Relations is a management phenomenon, involving two-way communication, a planned action, involving a form of social responsibility [2]. As such, corporate identity is a mixture of communication, symbolism and behaviours [3]. Related to public information is a concern with reputation, why bother to show the organisation in anything other than the very best light? If reputation or the measure of positive regard follows from a belief or beliefs and opinions someone has about another person or product, and then reputation management is fundamental to the success of an organisation, and represents a core tangible and intangible asset. A good reputation (which is the aim of Public Relations) can create barriers to competitive threats, secure competitive advantage, provide a strategic value through relationships, and underpin financial value. Four main publics – employees, customers, investors and communities [4]. According to Edelman, there are four main reputational challenges in contemporary Public Relations. These are: The rise of new media (including social media, and PCDs – personal communication devices); the increasing dispersion of authority (citizen journalisms, and the democratisation of information access); growing expectations of responsibility (sustainability, reducing environmental footprint, health and safety); and increasing governmental regulation [5]. These are trends observable in Western society at large.

Organisations use reputation to build trust in its publics and stakeholders and try to persuade public to change attitudes or behaviours to those that are favourable towards the organisation. Listening and feedback are important components of two-way symmetrical Public Relations. As such authentic relationships, involve dialogue and conversation, which enables each side to influence and shape view of other, and to determine the extent of whether they are willing to alter their behaviour and to accommodate the needs of others. Public Relations is primarily informed by processes which span four areas or stages – research and insight (what are the issues, what are the organisational challenges; which are the publics what are the threats and opportunities to reputation); secondly, planning which involves problem solving and building relationships, and objectives setting; and an implementation phase in which the plan is carried out through a variety of communication channels; and evaluation which measures the effectiveness of the activities and examines how well the campaign achieved what it set out to do.

Table 1. Showing public relations branches and their media [6]

Issues management	Legal and technological impact on an organisations
Criticism management	Clear messages in changing situations
Brand management	Communicating using brand guidelines
Publicity promotion	Customers are encouraged to use services
Public affairs	Communication on behalf of a publically owned body
Not for profits	Third sector charity groups
Media relations	Communicating with journalist, specialists from local, national, and trade media.
Celebrity Investor Relations	Communicating on behalf of a famous person
Publications Management	Media processes and digital delivery mechanism
Event Management	Organisation and supervision of media and sponsorship events
Copy Writing	Information delivered through a variety of channels

Corporate Public Relations involves internal employee communication, communicating with employees to align cultures and values; public affairs which involves opinion formers, politicians, lobbying, investor relations, financial organisations, individual; and corporate responsibility which involves local community and new influencers / community relations, and online communities. The tools used by Public Relations are manifold and include: Advertising; sales and incentives; direct marketing; direct selling; licensing and merchandising; brand management; social media; sponsorship and hospitality events. Public Relations are concerned with the media environment, the political system, the economic system and the level of development, activism, infrastructure, and culture of the myriad means by which we transmit information. Historically speaking, Public Relations may have originally arisen with the use of the cuneiform script and with Roman graffiti, which proliferated in the markets of street sellers in pre-Christian Europe, and the Middle-East. In contemporary society, it was not until 1970 that it was established professionally at the organisational level. As it expanded,

Public Relations became concerned with concepts such as ethnocentrism and diversity (seeing one perspective though being aware of more), cultural relativism (discounting cultural differences) and with strategic communication for different types of organisational use including establishing and maintaining relations with relevant publics. Public Relations are a subset of business and social relations within globalisation.

The international concerns of Public Relations are those that affect anyone with a public conscience or whom endorse corporate responsibility – for example, concerns with health and safety, environmental pollution, security, human rights and latterly sustainability and global warming within organisations -- as well as how good they are at what they do. Public Relations spans human resources, community relations, trade, and media relations as interactive spheres within business and society and the working orbit of client or organisation. Despite the fact that, as Srivamesh (2003) suggests, Public Relations is characterised by "media control, media differentiation, and media access," nevertheless the popular perception is that it is synonymous with media relations and with reputation management [7]. One of the central issues of reputation management is the aim to separate Public Relations from media relations and impression management from fact. Media relations and impression management are concerned with the way in which organisations, individuals and corporations relate and deal with their publics. But as Sean Lenehan notes: "*PR is not advertising.*"

GLOBALISATION – A DISPERSION OF MEANING?

The globalisation of Public Relations as a business service is a reality, not a myth, but that does not mean that each group or entity represents its own interests in the way that it would necessarily want to. Public Relations practitioners do not distort reality but put the concerns with representing their client and organisation in the best possible way. The reasons why Public Relations might be seen as being an illusion, and attract scepticism amongst a lay public is that Public Relations is 'packaged truth' and as such it is easily remembered and sometimes readily forgotten by both stakeholders and publics. It is 'easily forgotten' because it is there to **solve** a problem, to bridge a communication gap, to fulfil market needs, and therefore as open to the cycle of demand and consumption as any other informational 'product'.

There is renewed interest in Marshall McLuhan's media theory. McLuhan's predictions of the influence of technology on communication in the latter quarter of the 20th and beginning of the 21st centuries have been influential. In his famous statement, 'the medium is the message' McLuhan's (1961) point was that technology itself might have no moral content rather that the vehicle of communication also constitutes the properties of its content. A light bulb, for example, exists for the single purpose to create light when an electric current flows through it – it provides a signal and carries out a function to create light but does not itself communicate anything other than its function. However, to expand the metaphor further, McLuhan argued that future media might even extend the medium of consciousness. As he stated in 1962:

> The next medium, whatever it is – it may be the extension of consciousness – will include television as its content not as its environment, and will transform television into an art form. A computer as a research and communication instrument could enhance retrieval, supersede mass library organisation, and retrieve the individuals' encyclopaedic function and . . . speedily tailor data of a saleable kind [8]

McLuhan anticipated a development like the Internet that would revolutionise peoples' lives from an informatics perspective, both enabling and complexifying Public Relations practices and the possibilities for communication and mis-communication amongst clients, organisations and stakeholders.

Public Relations and maintaining reputation matters because good reputation is synonymous with the ability to do business. When the public perceives an organisation or person to be effective, doing their job well, to be rewarding or simply easy to deal with, they are more likely to want to do business with them and to continue to do so. However, reputation is also fickle and may easily degrade through poor service or an event, which lessens the organisation's business capability or their media image of business ethics and corporate responsibility. These concepts have existed for as long as people have been doing business but have characteristics that are synonymous with those of the age. As Abraham Lincoln suggested, "character is like a tree and reputation like its shadow. The shadow is what we think of it; the tree is the real thing" [9]. A truism of reputation management is that even the best salesperson *cannot make a bad product good* and it is all too easy to confuse communication with behaviour and performance. However, what good reputation management can do is make an average organisation or company better, and it can also limit the damage for an organisation, that makes a mistake. As Mark Twain once put it: "[a]lways acknowledge a fault frankly. This will throw those in authority off their guard and give you opportunity to commit more." Any competent Public Relations practitioner and many clients will learn from past mistakes and will not make them again, and so it is with organisations – responsible organisations anyway. Therefore, while communication objectives should be in synchronicity with business objectives, they are distinct from them [10]. In business, you really do need to 'walk the talk'. Furthermore, businesses are dynamic and interactive and human communication is a form of 'open system.' A Public Relations practitioner is both shaped by environments and is a shaper of environments. Thus as, Doorley and Garcia state, "the challenge of professional Public Relations is dealing with truth, falsity and ambiguity, and managing through the muddle with integrity" [11]. Even the worst situation in which no-one seems co-ordinated with anyone else is salvageable by professionalism and sticking to a story that most closely resembles reality. Therefore, the integrity of a Public Relations practitioner is premised on the extent to which he or she can exercise professional judgment and promote statements that are true and beneficial to the client [12].

In today's globalised market Public Relations involves new media technologies that proliferate from the engineering possibilities of satellite communication, optical fibre and the internet. Public Relations is dynamic and the active role of business and the opportunities and challenges to it

[13]. Consequently, the McLuhan 'global village' characterised by convergence and divergence is very much a realisable experience in the contemporary business world. Divergence involves the retention of the uniqueness of individual societies confronting globalisation. Without originality and without local adaptations, homogenisation results and media is degraded of meaning [14].

A professional communicator engaged in reputation management for an organisation does not promote statements that are harmful (except, for example, disclosure in investment markets for ethical reasons). Whereas an ethical communicator is concerned with telling the truth, an unethical communicator might be unconcerned as to whether a statement is true or not, or if a statement is known to be untrue, to be unconcerned in correcting it [15]. There are five facets to media relations: corporate media relations, (which spans the whole organisation), media relations (stories featuring individual products), marketing Public Relations (which is the coverage of company, products, issues and people) and financial media relations. Each has a distinct function in a geographic region or company [16]. In theory the press can ask any question they want but does not have a right to know certain items of information – proprietary information, personal information, or information that is not fully developed or information that would threaten security, which can in turn be withheld [17].

Furthermore, Public Relations is a two-way exchange, a symmetrical form of communication. A distinction is made between so-called 'advertorial' styles of news (paid for press releases), news that is in the public interest and syndicated by professional journalists, and 'propaganda' which the distortion of truth or the focus on a contextually disengaged proposition for the benefit of an organisation or entity in a one-way communication message. The latter being associated with dictatorial regimes. However, importantly, Public Relations is controlled information, it is moderated communication. As Heather Booke stated ironically: "Public Relations is at best promotion or manipulation, at worst evasion and outright deception. What it is never about is a free flow of information." In the dissemination of news and organisational press releases, it is also important to distinguish scientific facts (which are independently verifiable and have a transcendental truth-value) from political facts, which may accord with the majority point of view independently of its truth-value (for example believing the world to be flat rather than hemispherical). Political facts can sometimes be termed 'fake news' or 'alternative facts'. The tension between the dialectic exchange of facts engendered from independent, neutral, professional news journalism, political journalism, scientific journalism, and citizen journalism, is a four-way competition in the modern western society.

Table 2. Showing Strata of communication types [18]

Characteristic	Press Agency	Public Information	Two-way asymmetric	Two-way symmetric
Purpose	Propaganda	Dissemination of information	Scientific persuasion	Mutual understanding
Nature of communication	One-way; complete truth not essential	One-way; truth important	Two-way imbalanced effects	Two-way balanced effects
Communication model	Source to receiver	Source to receiver	Source to receiver with feedback	Group to/from group
Where see it applied most	Sports, theatre	Government, non-profit, business	Competitive business; agencies	Regulated businesses, agencies

Public Relations is also concerned with both positive and negative disclosure (the 'reach' or distribution of information). A first principle is that a client or organisation should act in compliance with laws and regulations. In most corporate or professional contexts, disclosure relates to whether information should be released [19]. The basis of Public Relations, aside from relationships and networking and communication is reputation – the stock of positive regard or credit that an organisation has with its clients, stakeholders and audiences. When an organisation becomes concerned with its own reputation and monitors its interactions with stakeholders, clients and media, it engages in reputation management. A basic formula is as follows:

Publication Relations = Networking and Relationships + Communication + Reputation

An important function of Public Relations is to allay rumour or 'grape-vine' communication which is (the) importance (of the news item) multiplied by ambiguity (the extent to which it is known, understood or misunderstood) [20]. Hence, when the activities of the organisation are factored in to the 'rumour mill' it is possible to arrive at an approximate formula of reputation as being the sum of constituency images (or news items), plus (organisational and stakeholder) performance and behaviour, plus communication (across the organisation and between stakeholders) [21].

Characteristics of the Information Environment

Thus, a central activity of Public Relations is the representation of a client – a person, company or entity to its constituency or market. It follows that a local event may take place in a globalised medium. Globalisation is defined as the "[i]ntensification of world-wide social relations which link distant localities in such a way that local happenings are shaped by events occurring miles way" [22]. Earth's land surfaces are divided into national (and international) territories, whereas globalisation refers to social, economic, cultural and demographic processes that constitute national activities within national territories, but which also transcend them. The performance of a nation is the work of the state – the guardian of national borders and the regulator of both citizenship and foreign policy. However, globalisation involves more abstract, less institutionalised and less intentional processes – technological developments in mass communication, global popular and mass culture, global finance and the environment [23]. This includes the plethora of the informatics of social media *Facebook, Twitter, Instagram* in the wider mediascape and the one-to-many-many-to-one rhizomal platform of information sharing on which they are based. One consequence is that while messages have in one sense become more proliferate, they have become less stable, more subjective to change, seeming to have a positional relevance where context is lacking. Such that there is a tension between globalisation that is seen as the impersonal and universal while localisation that is seen as being context specific and personal. These concepts and characteristics are competing, entwined and may overlap in what may seem to be the homogenisation of space, time and classification, freed from geopolitical context – an informational overlay. As Kearney states, globalisation is mediated by ". . . migration, commerce, communication technology, finance, tourism etc." [24]. Within the concept of globalisation, there are hyperspaces, which include airports, franchise restaurants and production sites detached from local reference, which all have homogenous universal qualities, and are also infospaces with advertising messages, the signified trace of mass production [25]. There are also hyperreal spaces of amusement parks, cinemas and art museums that consist of cultural representation and simulacra. As Appadurai (1996) states, the cultural space of globalisation includes ethnoscapes (the information that results from the migration of people through cultures and borders, a mobile diaspora of communities), technoscapes (the information that derives from the cultural interactions derived from technology), financescapes (the information that is part of the cross-border movement of capital, and currencies between nation-states), mediascapes (which represents the information derived from the mediascape, or the ubiquitous but ever-changing flickering world of mass media, and the electronic production and dissemination of signs symbols and communications) and ideoscapes (the tensions between and amongst the global flow of ideologies) [26].

Globalisation and Communication

As processes of industrialisation got underway the early expansion of capitalism fed off pre-existing spatial differences between capitalist and non-capitalist formations in which there was a deeper accumulation of value from peripheral communities subsumed to core areas, which, in turn, transformed developing communities. Industrial centres tended to create satellite dependencies. However, in the post-industrial era the now expansive power of capitalism to differentiate has seemingly gone full circle and is falling back onto itself, imploding cores and reducing the differences from peripheries [27]. There has been a large shift from manufacturing into service industries in the developed world. The result is more a rhizomal network of increasing urbanisation. Communication is rarely simply in the 'push-pull' model of former mass media but increasingly digitised, multiplex, banded.

Media items are propositions about society and convey a description of society's current state, fulfilling peoples' needs for knowledge and monitoring of the world around them [28]. The media system exists as the reality it observes, or the system constructs reality as it constructs itself [29]. There are now considered to be four types of communities – those that are closed to others, single communities, autonomous political units, and communities that are globalised and inter-connected in scale and scope. Furthermore, there are two main models of globalization. The first is what Tomlinson (2008) calls the penetration of the mundane, formerly distinguished cultural referents into the ". . . local/globalizing media and communications technologies – television, mobile phones, email, internet, transformation of the local into the 'international' . . . cultures." [30] This model assumes that to communicate with modern technologies signals a homologous complicity with an international culture with a limited 'symbolic capital'. The other argument is that globalization involves the exposure of differences, corresponding there is an 'exposure differential' in which the greater a rarity becomes known the more demand is placed on its consumption or experience. This tends to produce a hyper-reality in which exaggeration is the new norm.

MEDIATED COMMUNICATION STYLES

If communication styles are culturally constructed and maintained [31] the understanding of 'world cultural patterns' can serve to enhance strategic planning and ease transition problems as Public Relations is used for positioning and re-positioning organisations within their markets and constituencies. As Ihator (2000) states, contrasting values for international Public Relations practitioners include:

- Individualism vs collectivism
- High context (tacit knowledge) vs low-context (explicit knowledge)
- The degree of media independence and freedom from bias
- Cultural impact on media content and channels
- Orientation in time [32].

People derive their concepts and beliefs about identity from a variety of sources and activities. These may include an affiliated organisation or the immediate family; however in-group societies tend to be less assertive and governed by group norms – 'birds of a feather' and so on [33]. Thus, the culture of individualism within some contexts of globalisation (politics, economics and markets), is characterised by competitiveness and to some extent co-operation. Furthermore, differences between high and low context cultures may affect Public Relations strategies. As Hall (1976) states ". . . a high-context (HC) communication or message is one in which most of the information is either in the physical context or internalised in the person, while very little is in the coded, explicit and transmitted part of the message. A low-context (LC) communication is just the opposite; i.e., the mass of the information is vested in the explicit code" [34]. Communication in a high-context culture is more porous and may involve affirming past relationships. Cultures, which consume and produce a lot of information (industrialised and post-industrialised cultures), tend to see time also in commodity terms. Time can be considered to be monochromic (doing one thing) or polychromic (doing many at once). For 'generation Z' or the children of the early 21st century, there are large-scale problems, which include global warming, over population, resources, and the potential for conflict.

GLOBAL COMMUNICATION

Global issues need not necessarily be negative but involve people with perceived common interests beyond national interests, involving global interactions between state and non-state partners, global media and possibly the formation of world public opinion in the reputation management of individuals, groups, organisations, nations, and transnationals [35]. The instantaneity of new media technologies should not be under-estimated in its effect on the reaction time of the Public Relations practitioner, and the ability of informal information to spread fast. Public Relations is also about how information is communicated through time and space and is accelerated to an instantaneous level, as the result of delayed or prolonged deliberation on decision making. There is a need for multi-cultural understanding -- culturally astute cosmopolitanism which is sensitive to multicultural and international nuances. For Hardt, (1979) ". . . [t]he study of mass communication can make sense only in the context of a theory of society; thus questions of freedom and control of expression, of private and public spheres of communication and of a democratic system of mass communication must be raised as part of an attempt to define the position of individuals in contemporary industrialised western societies" [36]. Through the effects of globalisation, there is a complex diffusion of ideas, information, capital and people across national boundaries. These may entangle local and global entities and identities – in multiple possibilities. As Pal and Dutta (2008) suggest, with the "disappearance of time and space as materialised and tangible dimension to social life" [37]. It is necessary for Public Relations practitioners to communicate quickly, accurately and with empathy among a variety of stakeholder groups. In a globalised world, there is a fragmented hyperactive network of communication and information flow, which characterises the interplay of media representations. Public Relations practitioners and theoreticians need to be sensitive to the entwined flows of identities, ethnicities, information, technologies, media, commodities that articulate the roles of power, structure, agencies and symbolic exchange, which are distributed in and among, ethnicities, infoscapes, technologies, media, and commodities in the transnational cultural milieu [38].

Chapter 2

'When to Be Exact and When to Be Aspirational': Messaging Focus

'People do not buy goods and services. They buy relations, stories and magic' – Seth Godin

You are a manger in a busy store and you have a zealous younger staff member who is eager to impress and wants to know all the facts and figures about the company. One morning as you are just settling in some administration tasks, the staff member asks you, exactly how many sales you want her to make today? Because she wants to beat the 'company record'. You pause and reflect and hold your arm out with your palm towards him as if gesturing to explain, '[t]his company works on the principle, that what goes around comes around and everything will happen in good time.' Your staff member frowns and says 'I better get to it then!' but you can tell that she is frustrated with your answer. You are sorry that you have given an open-ended response but you wanted the staff member to recognise that the store thrives on genuine engagement; and customers do not want staff members jumping down their throats.

Communication theorists generally regard the reduction of uncertainty – or disambiguation -- as a key factor in business communication [39] but in Public Relations, particularly during and after crises, there is always ambiguity, and the crisis manager and Public Relations strategist strive to disambiguate the market situation to the advantage of the organisation, and focus on the specific message that the organisation wishes to communicate (but which ironically may be itself be ambiguous - sometimes). Certainly, ambiguity in the business environment has positive and negative qualities. Everyday positive features of ambiguity in business language include the use of metaphor to explain, promote cohesion and provide inspiration, however, this may be contrasted with negotiating and contracting in which the elimination of uncertainty is a necessary condition before forming any business agreement. This in turn may contrasted with the purposive use of strategic ambiguity to inform, disambiguate and provide meaning. Ambiguity in the workplace will always exist when there are two or more people engaging in symbolic interaction to exchange information [40]. The sources of ambiguity are multiple. Ambiguity can result from indecision, an intention to mean several things at once, or the fact that a statement may have different meanings. For Eisenberg (1984), ambiguity is engendered through "detailed literal language as well as through imprecise, figurative language" [41]. However, ambiguity itself is ambiguous. Ambiguity of meaning may be very independent of perceived ambiguity, which is a psychological variable, which may be different again from the ethical use of "strategic ambiguity" within an organisation [42]. As Eisenberg suggests, "ambiguity occurs in an organisation when there is no clear interpretation of a phenomenon or set of events. . . ambiguity can exist within the organization as a whole as well as within individuals" own cultural experience" [43].

Strategic Ambiguity within a Business Organization

Although some of our experiences with ambiguity may teach us that while being clear in communication is a worthy goal, there exists a body of thought which argues that clarity in communication is 'non-normative' and not a sensible standard against which to assess individual or organisational effectiveness. Rather, ambiguity can be seen as a continuum between exact understanding and nonsense. We are more likely to achieve rapport with someone who communicates with us such that we can understand them; and others are more likely to achieve rapport with us if we can communicate so as to be understood. For dependable patterns of action and independent initiatives to coexist in the business environment, a consensus of meaning is sufficient but not necessary. However, as Salazaar (1996) states, ambiguity may have an effect on group strategy for decision-making for " … under conditions of uncertainty and ambiguity, individual decision makers engage in search processes to better define the problem confronting them … [S]earch involves assessing information regarding alternatives, establishing criteria, and examining outcomes and payoffs associated with those outcomes" [44]. The process of searching can itself be creative but a risk is divergence unless clear parameters are set. A further response of strategic ambiguity is convergence. This occurs when people may share "fantasy themes or a rhetorical vision" which gives them a sense of identification with a shared reality [45]. Convergence may occur informally within an organisation and only tangentially be related to it, or more formally through Public Relations campaigns. As Mary Conley Eggert states: "*[a] success story without a name behind the endorsement is like an Indianapolis race car with its fuel gauge on empty. If you want your success story to genuinely impress a prospect, it has to make real noise by naming names.*" Public Relations is fundamentally about people, and Public Relations practitioners are *peoples' people.* However, people are motivated either internal or external forces – money, fame, success. The people do the doing; if 'money makes the world go round', it is only because people want it turning!

In order to be able to adapt, Menz (1999) argues that an organisation needs to be able to effect "a continuous balance between adaptation and adaptability, between stability and flexibility" [46]. Furthermore, Eisenberg has argued that "strategic ambiguity" is essential to a business organisation in so far as it: Firstly, promotes unified diversity, for example, by contributing to group identity formation; secondly, facilitates organisational change, by signalling aspirational values, and/or; thirdly, amplifies existing source attributions and preserves privileged positions by "mythologizing leadership roles" or minimising commitments that are difficult to break [47]. As Gail Kelly notes: "In this digital age, there is no place to hide behind Public Relations people. This digital age requires leaders to be visible and authentic and to be able to communicate the decisions they've made and why they've made them, to be able to acknowledge when they've made a mistake and to move forward, to engage in the debate."

Ambiguity and Organisational 'Climate'

The positive view of some levels of strategic ambiguity within organisations is partly a response to internal recognitions and partly a result of the desire to achieve external objectives. For example, employees might be enthused by a successful advertising campaign depicting their business as operating successfully if they could see it is congruent with already existing values.

The role of the recognition of value to the ascription of 'cognition' to the worker in an organisation in historical terms is a relatively modern concept. Most efficient and productive workplaces today will value some degree of workplace autonomy within organisational structures. Whilst the desire for accountability will remain the predominant factor, as Eisenberg suggests, there is a shift in most progressive workplaces to seeing organisational participants as "thinking individuals with identifiable goals" [48]. In order to distinguish ambiguous communication firstly from 'interference and noise' and secondly, from disruption to channels of communication, it must be understood that "complex systems are not dominated by linear and causal relations but by non-linear ones" [49]. The difficulty here is that non-linear relations may be a cause, by-product or indeed causally irrelevant to the creation of ambiguity but *are* seen as relevant to its perception. In ambiguous workplace situations, it is difficult to distinguish between cause and effect because frequently communication may be attributable to the organisational 'climate' rather than a defined source.

Within many organisations, the role of manager is seen to be taken by people who are skilled 'symbolic communicators'. Often managers use language effectively because it is a by-product of political, dramaturgical and language skills necessary for organising resources and people. Competent communicators may use "strategic symbols" to accomplish their goals, but the communicative change of this language use may not always be open or clear [50]. As Shelby Ray puts it: *"[y]ou may have a method of doing things one way, but someone has a preference of you getting it done another way. You have to be flexible in this industry and learn quickly."*

Furthermore, as objectives change, the goals of communicators may also change. Meaning is rarely unitary or consistent, and often people in the workplace have multiple and sometimes conflicting goals, which they orient towards. As people in organisations confront multiple situational requirements, they may respond to communicative strategies, which do not always minimise ambiguity. As Eisenberg comments, the "climate" of a business may also shift from an ideological adherence to clarity towards one of a contingent strategic orientation; this may or may not be communicated amongst the various levels of the organisation [51]. In any organisation, there may be three or more levels of communication reflecting different uses and tolerances of ambiguity. At lower operative levels, there is often tighter control over ambiguity than at middle-management level, whereas higher levels of management may use both ambiguous and non-ambiguous language in everyday language use.

Eisenberg compounds the complexity of the use of strategic ambiguity in organisational communication by suggesting that while explicit communication may be a concept of cultural assumptions, it is "not a linguistic imperative" [52]. People will vary their language along a continuum of explicitness and indirection, depending on how they may "read" another person's desires, aims, or understandings [53]. Ambiguity may thus be seen as a resource of language which may intentionally or otherwise be employed to strike a balance between being understood, "not offending others and maintaining a self-image" [54]. Furthermore as Salazar suggests, in decision-making situations characterised by minimal ambiguity in which "members are homogeneous" with regard to information and the "task is not novel," communication is likely to play a minimal role [55]. This may be compared with organisational situations of high ambiguity in which the motivation to "persuade, exchange information, check for errors in reasoning" – all the necessary factors for effective decision-making – will be stronger [56].

Frequently any communicated message will deviate from a hypothetical ideal. Ambiguity may be defined in terms of "message attributes" (lack of specificity, abstract language, absence of a course of action) and receiver interpretation (perceived equivocality of the message) [57]. Eisenberg argues that the concept of an ideally clear message is misleading in so far as clarity is a relational variable a continuum which "reflects the degree to which a source has narrowed the possible interpretations of a message and succeeded in achieving a correspondence between intentions and interpretation of receiver" [58].

In a turbulent business environment in which there are many impacting external or internal variables, ambiguous communication is a "rational method" used by communicators to orient towards multiple goals [59]. In any organisation there are conflicts between centralisation and decentralisation, the individual and community, self-determination and security, as such strategic ambiguity may promote unified diversity. The issue of divergent goals may be manageable not necessarily by consensus but through the "development of strategies to preserve and manage differences" [60]. A variation of strategic ambiguity is "equivocal communication". This is described as "non-straightforward" communication, which may be ambiguous, tangential, or evasive. Equivocal communication is usually indicative of avoidance and is used when all other forms of communication might lead to negativity [61].

In complex business organisations with many members, and multiple organisational values and interpretations, a sense of unity may by derived from points of symbolic divergence. Ambiguity may be used strategically to encourage creativity and guide against the acceptance of "one standard way of viewing organisational reality" [62]. Sometimes the role of leaders is to provide meaning for followers. The language required may be abstract, evangelical, and even poetic.

AMBIGUITY IN JOB-RELATED MESSAGES

Discounting a normal range of tolerance for communication ambiguity, Krayer and Bacon (1984) infer that differences in the perception of ambiguity in a stimulus message is "significantly related to differences in role ambiguity perceived by the worker on the job" [63]. This positive correlation between communication ambiguity and role ambiguity means that reductions in perceived communications ambiguities can be achieved through diminished role ambiguities. As role ambiguity may cause stress and organisational dysfunction, the knowledge that role ambiguity and communication ambiguity are correlated may mean that a reduction in the former may result in a reduction in the latter. Thus, the ambiguity of job-related messages may reduce in an organisation in which roles are clearly defined.

Pickert (1981) has described how the ability to provide a solution for an ambiguous task may enact decentration (or 'reversibility', the ability to focus on two or more aspects of a problem simultaneously and relate them together) in two ways [64]. Firstly, to interpret and respond to an ambiguous communication may involve the consideration of another person's point of view (involving concrete operational thought). As the respondent may realise that they lack information they will then ask questions, social decentration may follow as the logic of the problem presented is considered but also the responses of other interpretants [65].

Furthermore, cognitive dissonance may be the result of communication in the business organisation as the result of unexpected appropriation or blame or simply changing market-circumstances. Dissonance occurs as the result of an unexpected correlation between concepts or events, which may produce tension or stress as the result of a perceived need to change (for example, either attitudes or behaviours). The overriding consequence of cognitive dissonance is the desire to reduce it; however, in the extreme this may produce “situational avoidance” [66].

Piotrowski (2005) outline 10 principles that provide a rule of thumb for managing ambiguity in the business environment [67]:

- Organise your thoughts Maintain a professional attitude
- Refrain from making judgments about others
- Keep an open mind
- Don’t make assumptions or jump to conclusions
- Keep emotions in check
- Be slow to take offence
- Give others the benefit of the doubt
- Keep control of yourself
- Ask what your immediate purpose is, what is the scope of the problem, what are the constraints or your response?

Following these 10 principles may alleviate some, but probably not all, of the ambiguity associated with job-related messages. Other strategies for reducing uncertainty involve checking perceptions by observing, interacting or asking questions of others [68]. You can also analyse your own impressions, recognising your own role, avoid early conclusions as well as checking perceptions by describing what you see or hear and seeking confirmation [69].

Ethical Uses of Strategic Ambiguity

As Eisenberg (1984) suggests, the uses of ambiguity within organisations are multiple but coalesce around issues relating to group leadership [70]. If used creatively and relatively benignly, strategic ambiguity can achieve organisational goals in an ethical manner. It can be used to provide inspiration that will imprecisely guide a group towards a desired aspiration, lead organisational change, or motivate productive organisational behaviour. Further identifiable benefits of strategic ambiguity include: holding strained relations together, allowing a group to employ a single voice, facilitating change, allowing for adaptation, creating durable meanings, maintaining standing and 'character insurance', avoiding costly commitments, and preserving future options or courses of action [71].

Moreover, at an interpersonal level strategic ambiguity can: Firstly, facilitate relational development; secondly, control what people share of private opinions, beliefs, and avoid conflict; thirdly, act as a buffer of deniability (essential to the moderation of different views); and fourthly, provide a useful compromise between known and unknown. However, it is necessary to stress that a distinction needs to be made between strategic ambiguity used at an interpersonal level and taking 'strategically ambiguous' communication personally. The latter may be ethically inadvisable in circumstances in which relationship needs conflict with organisational expectations or protocols.

Here it is relevant to make a distinction between the use of strategic ambiguity in Public Relations campaigns that reflect realities of the business' operating environment and those, which seek to conceal or present alternative realities. There are no uniformly established ethical guidelines but today's society of social media prolificacy is finely attuned and potentially rapidly mobilised to expose major discontinuities in issues of public interest.

Krohn (1994) has argued that the Sapir-Whorf-Korzybski hypothesis may be applied in the context of training business communication students in ethical practice by discouraging words that denote violence and including general semantics training [72]. Despite the view that, "...the very act of communicating in the social context of a business culture implies an ethical basis, a respect for persons" [73], the fact that there is a lack of a common framework for deciding what is ethical language use in business practice tends to detract from the concept that openness in communication is a factor which affects business performance [74].

Ambiguity and Crisis Management

As Ulmer and Sellnow (2000) have suggested, crises in which there is a high degree of organisational ambiguity can result in benefit to the organisation if handled effectively. In crises, the idea is to "reduce communication ambiguity" [75]. One of the difficulties in reducing ambiguity in crises is that businesses need to maintain the support of many groups including customers, employees, stockholders and regulatory agencies. Efficient communication is therefore essential, since reducing contradictory information lessens the ambiguity of crises and allows for planning a way ahead. Here 'reductionism' may be useful – reducing a problem to its smallest parameters. In this respect, ambiguous communication may allow "divergent interpretations" to coexist and diverse groups to work together [76]. However as Ulmer and Sellnow (2000) suggest, "strategic ambiguity" may be ethical when it involves conveying complete and unbiased information and unethical when biases or gaps in knowledge are evident [77]. Ultimately, the discourse of business communication may be accepted or rejected on the grounds of reasonableness. Thus understanding the ethical complexities of 'losing balance' in the communication with relevant stakeholders is important in understanding and rectifying communicative practices to resolve ethical tensions in a crisis. Cheney (1991) observes that understanding ambiguity may lead to a decentring of the self within the organisation by making the worker view themselves as a 'subject' within a system they do not fully understand. In normal organisational communication, not all puzzles have to be solved straightaway [78].

Ambiguity and Risk

Ambiguity can be understood as being similar to economic 'risk', a term used to describe a situation in which an investment is made but of which the outcome is uncertain. In some forms of risk, outcomes are uncertain but probabilities are known. In others, termed "economically ambiguous," the probabilities of uncertain outcomes are unknown [79]. People prefer to take 'risky' decisions rather than ambiguous decisions, which suggests that people are averse to making decisions in "low information environments" [80]. Furthermore, neuroeconomic studies by Ellsburg (1961) [81] and Hsu, Bhatt, Adolphs, Tranel and Camerer (2005) have discovered evidence for brain regions preferentially activated by ambiguity (the *frontal cortex* and *amygdale*) and risk (the *parietal cortex* and *striatum*), implying that they may be separately encoded in the brain [82]. Therefore, there is physiological evidence that the human brain processes ambiguity and risk in different ways.

AMBIGUITY IN ACQUISITIONS AND MERGERS

Risberg's (1997) study of ambiguity and communication in cross-cultural business acquisitions reveals that the process of company acquisitions and mergers is often for the acquired companies a threatening experience. One reason is that the present and future frequently become ambiguous and uncertain. Problems are seen to develop from lack of sufficient information or a function of different values [83]. Therefore, consistency of information between acquiring and acquired companies is important in creating meaning out of uncertainty. Differences in organisational cultures can be due to differences in ethnicity, gender, nationality or ideology or subcultures with conflicting assumptions [84]. Risberg suggests that three perspectives may be used to study corporate culture: the "integrative perspective, the differential perspective, and the ambiguity perspective" [85]. The integrative perspective emphasises commonalities between organisational cultures; whereas, the differential perspective stresses inconsistency and lack of consensus; the business culture is seen as either harmonious or conflicting. The ambiguity perspective combines aspects of each.

Many of the failures in acquisitions and mergers are due to the ambiguities produced from cultural clashes. These occur when companies refuse to find commonalities and instead see differences. Unlike the integrative perspective the differentiation, perspective does not deny ambiguity; there may be different sub-cultures within any organisation. Multiple perspectives in any one organisation and a climate wholly of neither harmony nor conflict are more likely to be formed in an organisational culture viewed from an ambiguity perspective.

AMBIGUITY AND LEADERSHIP

Whilst most workplaces would have ideals of: security, community, respect, authority, and clarity in communication, in the era of social media, the worldwide web, globalisation and global warming, the pace of change within organisations has increased dramatically. Therefore, many organisations need to remain agile and responsive to changing internal and external environments. However, there is a fine line between the communication of organisational values and the communication of organisational change in which planning sometimes gives way to adaptation. As Amorium (2010) suggests, business organisations need to know who they are (how they are defined in their operations) and what they want (or want to become), because the "how of their plans will be a moving target" [86]. Clearly, visionary leadership and the ability to implement plans are on a continuum with variable points of intersection. Consequently, in times of organisational change, dealing with ambiguity is a leadership skill. Hooper defines the following characteristics of leadership skills [87]:

LEADERS

- Can effectively cope with change
- Can decide and act without having a total picture
- Aren't upset when things are up in the air

- Can comfortably handle risk and uncertainty and are future-orientated
- Handle volatility, uncertainty and complexity
- Identify threats and opportunities in business practice.

Thus, leadership skills for 'uncertainty' are desirable and may in fact be necessary qualities for the modern workplace. Leaders often attract praise or blame for their 'judgment' but suspension of judgment may in fact be more valuable in many situations in which ambiguity results from excessive uncertainty or change. On the other hand, clarity of communication may enhance or inhibit workplace anxiety. Mitzberg (2009) analyzes a growing trend he terms 'macro-leading', characterised by "leaders who manage by remote control, disconnected from anything except the big picture" [88]. However, the opposite trend of 'micro-managing' may also inhibit organisational direction and growth by dampening down necessary sparks of creativity.

For any leader in today's business market, opportunities and challenges must be appreciated from multiple viewpoints and not just seen as 'traits' to be expressed from a personal leadership bias. Often causes of conflict within an organisation are difficult to 'diagnose' from a single perspective. Thus, a leader's role must sometimes be to set reasonable goals and to 'disambiguate'. However, providing a clear direction, synchronising the motivations of others and communicating adjustments within an organisation may involve both clear instruction and ambiguities. Other qualities of a leader's toleration to ambiguity include listening well, thinking divergently, and the setting up of incremental dividends to reward the efforts of workers.

Anthony (2010) argues that complexity, sudden shifts in the basis of competition and global competitors are the "new norms" of constant change which face tomorrow's global leaders [89]. Whilst giving people more responsibility helps them refine skills, the acquisition of new skills as the result of ambiguous threats and challenges may also be a driver of business capability. Thus Anthony suggests rather than 'scaling' being a measure of success, giving leaders "smaller ambiguous challenges" may instead result in the acquisition of competencies necessary for climbing the corporate ladder [90]. Managers and staff may need to be trained to be able to use conflict management strategies effectively and deal with situations of ambiguity and uncertainty. This may involve deeper understanding of aspects of interpersonal communication or the uses of strategic ambiguity within an organisation. As Robbins (1993) points out, conflict may result from incompatibility over goals, differing interpretations of facts, disagreements about behavioural expectations, and from arguments over resources [91]. However, as Sayers (2005) suggests, sometimes conflict "cannot and should not be resolved" [92]. Whilst one strategy for dealing with ambiguity is simply to learn to 'tolerate' it, by gradual frequency and acclimatisation to exposure from the people who employ it, there is also a creative element in strategic communication, which can work to an organisation's advantage. To use strategic ambiguity takes confidence because it also contains a risk of indirect communication or that the audience simply will not understand it.

Many working environments may go through periods of structured antagonism in which general staff values of freedom may conflict with values of managerial control. Conflict may arise from semantic difficulties, misunderstandings, lack of information or information distortion. Skills that managers of ambiguity in business organisations require are: being able to reconsider boundaries of people's positions, thinking creatively to find new solutions, emphasising relatedness rather than polarising views, the willingness to work through any problem, and not necessarily to seek to end conflict but to "manage it properly" [93]. Whilst there may be an important practical consideration in maintaining clear and unambiguous communication in everyday procedural matters within organisations, when managed carefully, both tactical and strategic ambiguity can add value to an organisation's communication if used in an ethical manner. Finally, the best practical advice is that when language use seems interpersonally ambiguous, it is far better to interpret it positively than negatively. In responding to reputational challenges, there are twelve popular points for the Public Relations practitioner to follow:

- Know the organisation (what is its identity, what is its values, core mission?)
- Know your stakeholders and how others perceive the organisation – perform a risk assessment if necessary
- Monitor the media and business environment for organisational issues and stakeholder engagement.

Make a reputation management plan. Apply CRM methodology to the organisation. CRM stands for **Comprehensive Reputation Management,** which is a conceptual strategy to align behaviours and communications and measure, audit and manage reputation.

- Engage in dialogue – two way symmetrical communication, be open and honest
- Build relationships with stakeholders
- Make near objectives and far goals (SMART – specific measurable achievable, realistic, time referenced)
- Stay committed
- Embed Reputation Management across the whole organisation
- Behave ethically
- Stay positive, and be open to critique [94]

In adopting these dispositions, activities, practices and attitudes the Public Relations practitioner may work to build the reputation of an organisation and ameliorate setbacks in the development and maintenance of its corporate or organisational profile.

Chapter 3

'When I Used to Be You and You Used to Be Me': Negotiating Skills

'To establish oneself in the world, one does all one can to seem established there already' – Francois De La Rochefoucauld

Every bargain, deal and counter-deal that is struck; every time you talk with a family member about sharing the chores, or even a team of diplomats and negotiators meet to discuss the terms of an international trade agreement; people are using negotiation skills, as they argue for a position (or for their clients' position) and discuss the details of any dispute or commonality with the other party to the discussion. Negotiation involves five main factors, which are based on a set of concepts in the areas of problem analysis, interpersonal communication, personal goal setting, managing feelings and personal boundaries. This chapter will elucidate the contexts of negotiation skills and describe how negotiation skills can improve organisational communication and personal goals.

THE NEGOTIATION FRAMEWORK

Negotiation is the art and science of compromise. It is about trading alternatives between the partners of a dispute or transaction. The negotiation framework is comprised of a variety of factors. These include the problem analysis – deciding on issues confronting parties and the conflict that requires repair or the decision that needs agreement. Hence, it is important to determine the interests of the parties, finding common ground, and agreeing to discuss points of disagreement and finding resolution for them. Hence preparation before meetings is important, establishing a clear position, determining goals and areas for discussion, as well as the practicalities of where, when and how a meeting will take place. One of the most important conditions for good communication and negotiation within meeting is listening skills. Active listening is listening that requires a little more effort than ordinary listening where it's not so important if you miss one or two details, on the contrary active listening involves more effort and attentive ness of the other person or party. When a person or people listening actively, they read body language carefully, looking at the cues of non-verbal communication – is the other person or party open, confident and relaxed, or withdrawn, anxious and closed-off? Listening involves determining the salient points of the other person or party's perspective and their feelings and attitudes towards it, finding areas of agreement and discussing areas of difference, and determining when and how compromise between each other's position and needs can be made. What can you give up to agree with the other person or party, and what can the other person or party give up to agree with you?

Any engagement with others at least when there is a face-to-face encounter or meeting, involves cognitive and emotional considerations. For the most part to reach agreement, then it is better to keep focused on the facts, simply because it will be more helpful and prudent to obtain a better outcome if the main considerations are forefront in the meeting agenda. However, people are not simply objects and conversation has a context. Any human interaction will involve some form of emotion, intuition, or feelings. Emotions and feelings, although not always reliable, nevertheless do give us salient information about ourselves and about others. It is therefore a mistake to discount and disregard all of one's emotions when negotiating with others. However, consideration of emotions brings a qualitative depth and dimension to negotiation situations. Context is everything. Ask yourself whether the emotion you are feeling is derived from yourself or is it a reaction to someone else, it is a feeling generated from them or from you about them? How might it enable you to understand them and their motivation better? Keeping to the facts will give you a clear conversational path, but the emotional tones will help you consider how to 'walk the talk.' Hence, in many forms of face-to-face or video-conferencing meetings verbal communication and non-verbal communication can be involved in the negotiation framework setting. Prepare to be assertive and put your position, needs, and point of view across and but also be prepared to accept compromise. Collaboration and teamwork does not necessarily involve one side against another and your decision-making ability will come to the fore in determining how and when or to what extent an agreement can be formed. A good working relationship requires interpersonal skills, which includes the ability to persuade others of your point of view without manipulating them, of listening well, and attempting to communicate to reduce any misunderstanding and diminish any excess ambiguity. This will enable trust to be formed to that, rapport may be built and assertiveness and control over a situation or a potential future situation arising from the agreement can be made. Clarifying goals will make everyone aware of their viewpoint. Negotiation will enable you to discuss differences and find common ground. When the interests of all sides is considered, agreement may be reached and a decision made on establishing a mutual position or on implementing a course of action. Failing to agree will involve deciding to meet together to discuss differences. The negotiation can be conducted either formally or informally and at the risk of repetition – key skills are questioning, listening and clarifying between parties.

INTERPERSONAL SKILLS

Interpersonal skills are paramount in successful negotiation. Interpersonal skills involve the range of verbal and non-verbal communication behaviours that are involved in mutual exchange of information, thoughts, ideas, concepts, media and feelings between people, either face-to-face, in-groups, out-groups, or across distances. There are many factors involved in clear interpersonal communication. This involve learning to listen. Learning to listen is not just hearing but listening how something is being said or being spoken. It involves clarification and reflection. A key factor is being sympathetic to other peoples' misfortunes and congratulating them on their positive achievements and consoling them when hard times strike and the possibility for sympathy arises. It is important to empathise. Try to see things from others points of view. The two golden tenets of empathy and attempting not to be judgmental (unfairly judging others without sufficient knowledge) or to bring pre-conceived ideas about another party (without the necessary knowledge about them). It is useful try attempt to see a situation from another person's point of view. While not all meeting, negotiations will require encouraging roles, nevertheless affirming basic values of confidence by encouraging them will make them feel welcomed, valued and wanted. Mindful listening involves learning to listen to communicate effectively, don't say the first thing that comes into your head, rather, take a moment to pay close attention to what the other party is saying and what you say in response. It is important to aim for clarity. Increasing your mutual understanding can result from being as clear as possible in articulating your position. With this in mind, it is important to consider how your message might be seen clearly. Humour can sometimes lighten a situation to 'break the ice' or to find common ground despite points of difference – laughter brings people together. Laughing triggers endorphins, which relieve body stress. Above all, communicate and deal with people frontally, treat them equally, avoid patronising them. Try not to talk behind people's' backs. Always have the aim of resolving conflict. Learn to troubleshoot, to mediate, to encourage and to facilitate when advancing a particular point of view, or when representing a client or entity. Do your best to be friendly, and maintain a positive attitude. Remember to smile as smiling relieves stress and stress is a barrier to successful communication. If you cannot smile then just stay calm, even when others around you did not seem calm, or when you think they are making your stressed. Try to keep focused on the task, and only complain when necessary. Stress passes. The sun will shine again!

Personal Goal Setting

A part of preparation for negotiation either over the long or short term is personal goal setting. Personal goal setting is concerned with the aims of setting objectives, of establishing levels of motivation and of long, medium or short-term vision. Often our personal goals and large and undefined or small and yet still indistinct. Achieving goals depends for a large part on motivation. If your long-term goals seem too large then try to break larger goals into shorter goals. If you goals are financial, set yourself a task of deciding how much you want to earn? What do you need to do to achieve that level? What is the knowledge, ability or skill that you want to acquire? What sort of lifestyle do you prefer? Do you want to be a parent? What sort of partner would you prefer? Do you want a nuclear or extended family? Do you have the skills to cope with either? If motivation is half of the issue of learning how to deal with something, then attitude is another four-tenths. Ask yourself whether you have the necessary resolve. Do you have the right mind-set to achieve what you want? Will your mind set be understood and potentially shared by others to reach an agreement? Your goals and attitudes might include the general aim of making the world a better place. Can you achieve this everyday or is it a diffuse aim? Ask yourself what might be holding your back, or preventing you form achieving your aims. Try to make a short-term plan, and a medium-term plan and a long-term plan. SMART goals are desirable. SMART goals are specific, measurable, attainable, relevant and time-bound. It is a good idea to keep goals realistic and achievable. If your goals are easily achieved then try to make the next goal more difficult. If you goal takes too long then make the next one easier.

Managing Feelings

One of the most important considerations in negotiation is managing feelings. The importance of empathy in dealing with others is essential but nevertheless there is a realisation that feeling often go in cycles. One can transition between hurt, sadness and anger and feeling misunderstood is a common experience but in even a moderately successful negotiation it won't last. Always try to limit and control excess emotions. Although emotions and feelings can give us valuable information about ourselves and others at times, emotions and feelings if left unconsidered and unchecked can weaken our ability to solve problems or to handle change and reorganising, understanding and controlling feelings can be difficult. If you know how you feel you can get your feelings under control. It is important to remember that in general, if you cannot make something better, then do not make it worse. If you are too consumed by, your own feelings then put yourself in another person's shoes. Although it is true that emotions are useful and every emotion has a purpose, then put yourself in other person's shoes. There is power in the ability to manage emotions. Try to be an observer of your own feelings and remember although emotions can be powerful, emotions do not always equal actions.

Personal Boundaries

Personal boundaries are about knowing where you stand in relation to others and 'surviving' as a freethinking functioning communicator when you are presented with all kinds of information from people. Personal boundaries may be about understanding ambiguity and learning to tolerate conflict, indecision and knowing how to sort out what is valuable to you and what is not while maintaining confidence in another person's point of view. One of the first maxims of personal boundaries is knowing and naming your limits. You cannot focus on an issue or problem unless you are sure of where you stand. Hence, you need to know yourself well to know understand and be able to use or control your personal boundaries. It helps to be able to recognise and identify your physical, emotional and mental limits. Often one of the biggest obstacles to communicating with others is perceived or unconscious resentment, which might derive from being taken advantage of or from what another person has in relation to you. However, once you stop consciously comparing what one person or another has, does not really matter. This is one of the reasons that corporates and people may frequently talk in metaphors. Maintaining healthy boundaries does not require black and white dialogue and it can be direct (and an instruction or an imperative) or indirect (as in a metaphor, analogy or allegory). Controlling ones emotions from the self in relation to others is one of the hardest tasks required in maintaining healthy boundaries. A key maxim is Give Yourself Permission. Fear, guilt and doubt are large potential pitfalls, try to recognise them, put them in perspective and overcome them. In order to do this it is necessary to practice self-awareness, boundaries are about maintaining effect communications and relationships of self to others, and about respecting the positions and point of view of others. Often it is necessary and wise to consider the past, present and future in relation to boundaries with others. One of the most obvious problem areas is that family interactions can prevent people from seeing and preserving their boundaries, personal relationships tend to 'get in the way' of professional relationships by the form of interpersonal bias they lend themselves to. However, it also important in situations where personal boundaries need preserving to make care of the self a priority, to recognise the importance of feelings and to seek support to be assertive. Large accomplishments can come from small beginnings. Personal boundaries are like water in a vessel; they reach equilibrium but can easily change. Some ordinary boundary sharing may involve considerations of whether one gives of lends things – money, clothes, hospitality and so forth and important physical boundaries are those that pertain to personal space, such as the private body and the extent to which it is shared with others or concealed from them. Mental boundaries apply to one's thoughts, value and opinions, while sexual boundaries involve ideas of privacy and protection and the autonomy of partners. Spiritual boundaries relate to beliefs and experiences in relation to God, and emotional boundaries involve distinguishing between emotions and the responsibility for them, whether to reward or punish, blame or to accept blame, praise or accept praise. Emotional boundaries may also demarcate an imaginary line that separates you from others. Healthy boundaries also prevent you from giving advice and protect you from feeling guilty for someone else's problem. Internal boundaries are about the relationship you may enjoy with yourself, they can be thought of as a form of self-discipline and may change with healthy management. Setting effective boundaries is essential in negotiation. Firstly, prepare, think who can help you, and think what the other party want, how much you can give to them and what you require in return. Try to develop relationships and to express a willingness to engage in learning and to develop opportunities to progress and share with others. If necessary, find an experienced mentor. Set those goals!

Chapter 4

'DUDE! BE REASONABLE': TRUTH AND CREDIBILITY

'We're all naked so we better be in good shape' – Diana El-Azar

If you are new to the area, most people think that Public Relations is either an exercising in exclusive small talk, or a version of mass media that attempts to persuade through elicit techniques, some might pre-judge and believe it synonymous with brainwashing and propaganda. The truth is Public Relations is none of these. Public Relations is at its essence a dialogue, it is not a one-way exercise in information control but a two way dialectical 'conversation' frequently using a variety of media and communicating with either small or large audiences. However, the relationship of reputation management and Public Relations to 'truth' is one well worth exploring further. In either variety of the field, truth is something to be embraced rather than avoided. Almost any Public Relations practitioner will tell you that nine times out of ten, it is better to be upfront and honest in your declarations on behalf of a company or organisation that is experiencing crisis. Declare, apologise, and say what you are doing to rectify the situation and how you will change. If we look a little more closely at the theory behind the kinds of relationships to truth that Public Relations practitioners are engaged in, then they come to look similar to those in another branch of communication – narrative formation. This chapter will cast a lens on the kinds of relationship to truth bearing propositions that might be found in Public Relations and reputation management discourse.

What relationship do media statements hold to constructs of truth? Fiction is the term used to describe information or events that are not factual but rather imaginary of make believe. Non-fiction by comparison is narrative about factual events, observations or descriptions. A lie is a false statement that is made intentionally. A bluff is a feigned intention and differs from an exaggeration or hyperbole in that the latter is true only to a certain extent. These differ in turn from fabrication in so much as the latter is a statement made without knowledge of truth. A half-truth is a partly true statement that may contain a form of deception. Public Relations strategists need to keep in mind, a relationship with truth telling, as well as a responsibility to client and stakeholders.

However, it is true that in today's mediated world, there are many truths just as any two people may hold different opinions on a matter of fact. Although it is possible to look for authenticating sources, increasingly truth has become a 'relativized' concept, a concept relevant from the position of the asserter or the perceiver. Often truth is context dependent, and although the 'truth will out' as the adage states, finding truth is often a matter of perceiving 'shades of grey'.

The Public Relations Practitioner needs to be mindful of the various rhetorical devices, which both reveal and conceal truth telling. Relatedly described as a 'curious artifice' of legal reasoning, a legal fiction is defined as being a "false statement as a necessary component of a legal rule" [95]. Thus a legal fiction is similar to a literary fiction in that it shares two characteristics of the former, it is asserted with a complete or partial consciousness of the falsity and is regarded as having a utility – thus is only misleading when believed [96]. Put another way legal fictions are like statements of fact that are not always verifiable according to real world references. A legal fiction might be thought of as 'intangibles' like the doctrine of discovery – the Crusoean 'finder's keepers' that is of course replaced by concept of ownership, title, and by property rights. However, a separate category of legal fictions exists which is characterised by adherence to abstract concepts (such as sovereignty, for example) but which are not conventionally provable except by association or succession [97]. A third category of legal fiction are those of empirical legal error which have three characteristics: firstly, they are issues of cognitive processes (reliability of testimony); secondly, they involve individual beliefs (legal understandings of what rules are); and thirdly, they represent institutional relationships (constructions relying on legal intent). A fourth category of legal fiction is that of a legal rule made based on a false factual supposition; and a fifth is that of discredited legal regimes [98]. Legal fictions function and operate by applying legal rules to novel circumstances through analogy, equivalence, and suspension of disbelief [99]. The paradox of a legal fiction is that they are frequently not intended as being deceiving but are acknowledged false.

Parrhesia is the concept of 'asking for forgiveness for so-speaking', it is a reflexive assertion of an ontology that reinforces a kind of relational authenticity by modifying existing power relations, and which may present truth as being contradictory to the present state of affairs [100]. People might engage in parrhesia when they doubt the authenticity of their speech or that of others. The term may describe the annunciation of a dissonance between perceived and future understandings of representation, or where one or more statements may be fiction. In such a way, fiction is an advantage over truth for opening unexplored potentialities and thus has a proleptic function [101]. Truth/fiction is thus a kind of 'toolkit' for those involved in interventions in the present, involving transformative relationships. Parrhesia is an evocation of truths which: firstly have traction with reality; secondly, uncover latent forms of the present; thirdly, have potential future effects; fourthly, constitute a new form of reality; fifthly, are transformative and potentially subversive; and sixthly, are connected with ontologies of being [102]. According to Busch, fiction is 'what passes for truth' [103].

As Wojcik suggests a statement expressed by a sentence about fiction "has a truth value which is not dependent on any dynamic conditions or external changes" [104]. In constructing narratives it is possible to accept the possibility of real events, people or places depicted by author but not necessarily to think what is so described actually happened. Thus, arguably, some forms of truth are not very relevant to make ordinary common sense. While true, they may be indemonstrable and too outlandish to be of any use in reputation management or in explaining concepts to the lay public. There are four possibilities about fictional entities – that they are always false, always true, neither false nor true, or either false or true. A sentence can be grammatically correct but false, or if always true lacking in informative value. Thus, fiction (as distinct from fact) may be characterised by four factors: firstly, it retains a truth-value secondly, it avoids ontological commitment; thirdly, it remains semantically and contextually justifiable; and fourthly, it can be about itself (metafictional) [105].

So asking what relationship those who use language publically hold to the truth is more complex than it first appears. Accuracy, consistency, validity and relevance are all tenets of truth telling statements yet because, for example, fiction writers recount things that are untrue, but do not claim them to be true, they cannot be held up as liars. In Public Relations it is better to tell the truth in a way that is most advantageous to your client, or to describe a version of events that is not untrue. However in the catholic tradition *mendaicum iocosum* (the lie of fiction and amusement) is distinguished from *mendacium officiosum* (to gain a good or protect from harm). Public Relations will rarely be poetry but sometimes a great outcome can come from an unexpected source. Francis Bacon referred to poetry as *'vinum daemonum'* – 'because it filleth the imagination; and yet, it is but with the shadow of a lie' [106]. The implication is that some may regard fiction as a trope of a lie [107]. So, in order to be clear, it is also relevant to look at forms of lying (or untruth telling), of which there are several. Firstly, the claim that the following events actually occurred (when they didn't); that A is really B (when it appears not to be); that A possesses a privileged authority; that clever manipulation of words reveals an analogous relation (when truth of relation is unknown); and the use of names and pseudonyms are forms of lies or the telling of untruths whether intentionally or not [108]. The relation a fictive story can be instructive (narrative, metaphoric use of expository mode or device; assertive trope); feigning or embellishing, creating, and describing is also instructive) [109]. But if you do use elements of fiction in Public Relations narratives, make sure that they embellish what is known to be true, in order to make the meaning come across in a more palatable way. It is part of human memory, imagination and reason that despite the idea of a real world being apprehensible to our senses what we begin to describe inevitably creates fictions (rather than lies). As Heidi Sullivan notes: *"Way before "PR" or "marketing" came to be, humans were doing something both disciplines hold (or claim to hold) dear: telling stories."*

Fiction is the result of minds that possess both fact making and imaginative cognitive abilities. Although the Newtonian physicist might insist otherwise, the effects of postmodernism and experiments in the quantum world tell us that the truth is relative and perhaps fallible rather than absolute or certain. Fiction is also widely regarded as being an imitation of life, and a transformational experience. So no matter how much you stick to the truth, there will always be some elements of a narrative that are introduced, simply through the passage of time. Of course with fiction the difference between subjective and objective versions of the truth, allow the perceiver to lift the veil of truth from the living [110]. Consequently, fiction mediates between subjectivity and objectivity [111]. Allen (1996) defines 'evidence' as "any matter of fact, the effect, tendency or design of which is to produce in the mind a persuasion, affirmative or disaffirmative, of the existence of some other matter of fact' [112]. Furthermore, any assertion that is based on probability, carries an explanatory power, or has the power of resisting denial, is capable of drawing *'Makanjuola'* (a warranted direction) from a court, that is to say, there are some categories of statement which are more clearly recognised as factual, with truth-bearing properties, than others. In this context 'multiple hearsay' – that is at several persons of remove, is rarely admitted in court.

The real meaning of 'truth' may simply be that of faithfulness and constancy. The poet Samuel Taylor Coleridge's 'willing suspension of disbelief' captures neatly the dual action of engagement and disengagement that the reader of fiction must make – disconnection from the events of the outside world and immersion in the created world or revelation of an internal consistency in the fictional creation. Internal consistency is central to fact making too but has the added component of being faithfull to real world events. Coleridge's description from chapter fourteen of the *Biogaphia Literaria* was thus of poetic faith, awakening the mind's attention from the lethargy of custom or the 'film of familiarity'. In comparison, Stuhring (2011) questions the reliability of fictional narratives stating that the narrative of a work of fiction F is unreliable if N justifies wrong beliefs about what is the case in F. However, some narratives are just partially unreliable and lacking relevant information but not all narratives intend to deceive the reader by entertaining wrong beliefs about the fictional world [113]. That doesn't mean that we should view public relations narratives with suspician that they are fictional (or hiding or embellishing fact) but that we should be open to the possibility that events can be described from a variety of perspectives. Try to present the truth in the best way possible for your client!

If we delve behind the theory of narrative creation, Ramsden argues that fiction in the wider sense does shape the everyday world. He states that fiction can refer to the shaping of discourse (*poiesis*), to the use of imagination and the art of feigning, and to the establishment of systems within a text and how the text relates to the 'world'. Ramsden (2011) also points out that facts are mental constructs – concepts which have origins in empiricism and positivism and yet scientists depend on the social, discursive and epistemological context to give them meaning [114]. Within this context, verisimilitude is a property of fiction relating to its claim to authenticity, or the 'appearance of truth' within a text, again exhibiting the idea of internal consistency. Linguistic models can be derived from both factual and fictional frames of knowledge reference, neither of which can exist independently of the viewpoint of the narrator [115]. Ramsden (2011) further argues that there are two basic attitudes that relate art to life – a reductionist perspective which argues that art is grounded in real world events, and that of the formalist for whom art may figure as an artefact – an aesthetic experience and part of an autonomous realm [116] Fiction can thus be thought of as a process that fuses, imaginary or real events into a comprehensive totality which becomes an object of representation [117]. Thus, although fiction and factual writing are distinct, a writer or a reader can actualise fiction, explore the relationship between the actual and textual world but at the same time recognise that fiction will really become real fact [118]. So a Public Relations commentator might state a mixture of what they know and what they don't know but they won't present a view of events that differ from whatever is the topic of discussion.

However, it is a characteristic of human cognition that the make-believe can stand in for the actual or that a lie may also be believed, moreover, where does fact end and fiction begin or vice versa? This is evident, for example, in the construction of identity or in testimony – both of which involve representations [119]. Thus, it could be said that the relation between fiction and factual representation is one of degree – and furthermore, whilst an easy transformation between fiction and nonfiction can be suggested through poetic expression, it seldom in reality takes or has taken place [120]. However, it is possible that new cultural orders may be produced by making created worlds 'real' through metaleptic artistic and scientific processes, despite the fact that simulated beliefs in the integrity of a narrated worlds may lead to the defamiliarisation of meaning [121]. Readers of fiction and non-fiction simultaneously inhabit two different worlds with differing ontological valences. As Mikkonen (2006) suggests, ". . . a fictional text is essentially a literary non-referential narrative: it can refer to the real world but need not do it; the referentiality of fiction does not have to be accurate or exclusive. . . [f]iction either concerns itself mostly with textual actual worlds or with textual alternative possible worlds or may take a nonfactual possible world and describe it as if it were actual" [122]. Thus, however much it approaches the aspect of the real through the effect of transformation or of verisimilitude, or from some other device, fiction can never be taken for real. It might, like a legal fiction, be accepted for being so and be rejected at the same time.

The judgment or thoughts that individuals may have over legitimacy stem from their personal belief system, which is comprised of both global values and domain specific values [123]. However, it is also informed by wider contextual issues such as credibility of the industry, of constituent organisations, and of media [124]. Legitimacy is a 'recognition tool' and enabler because it allows the legitimate party and those who give them recognition to share resources. Legitimacy influences the norms and cognitive categories of a system, and some values are normative because they instantiate preferred goals and the means to achieve them [125]. However, other second-level beliefs are characterised as understandings that individuals have about a subject but may lack an emphasis on norms [126]. It can thus be said to be a form of attitude that involves the exchange of information, of personal values involving a "favourable or unfavourable" evaluation of a subject involving interconnected beliefs [127]. For Finch (2013), legitimacy is also defined as the acceptability of a subject to a social system but is distinguished from social evaluation concepts like status and reputation [128]. Finch (2013) explains that legitimacy can thus be seen as an attitude or a construct involving multi-dimensional evaluations that are pragmatic, moral, regulatory and cognitive [129].

Credibility signals its meaning through two influential characteristics, the content of message and the credibility of a source. Thus, the message content provide the information about a subject that is then compared to a relational criterion [130]. It is thus a concept that related to the believability of a source, a domain specific belief that is consistent with an understanding about a source context [131]. The main dimensions of credibility are considered to be expertise, honesty and the trustworthiness of a source [132]. People are more influenced by messages from a source they believe is credible. If a source is less credible, they are less influenced by it [133]. Public Relations commentators should above all be credible.

For Flangin et al., (2014), ratings are positively associated with product quality and purchase intention and people tend to average ratings, although they also tend to privilege a small number of ratings that become idiosyncratic [134]. The quality of the product may mediate a relationship between rating and purchase intention. In 2012 ecommerce constituted about four-percent of sales in the United States (some forty billion dollars annually), two-thirds of people made one purchase or more, and an even larger percentage, over ninety-percent, used the internet for commerce-related activities [135]. However, the fact remains that online commercial transactions lack some elements that have served to ensure credibility among exchange parties. There are varying 'patronage modes' which embody different levels of consumer risk for those separated from having a physical presence at a store, people need to assess the credibility on online information and the commercial trustworthiness of the medium [136]. Thus, for consumers, risks are whether they know they have selected the right vendor, brand, or mode of purchase, and how satisfied they have paid a fair price [137]. Therefore, the level of ambiguity around a commercial transaction is moderated by the amount of information that people find credible.

If problems with purchasing a product or service do occur then there are dimensions of fairness, justice or remedy that may influence customer's perceptions of recovery of service. These include distributive justice, which concerns perceptions about the organisation's efforts to rectify a problem (and achieve fairness of outcome). Actions can include replacements, refunds, and discounts on future purchases. Interactional justice – which focuses on fairness of the interpersonal interactions between employees, employers, clients and customers – empathy, friendliness, courtesy, cultural respect, and or apologies. Thirdly, procedural justice concerns the methods and processes by which the company organisation handles problems – accessibility, time, control and flexibility of response [138].

Word of mouth advice is perceived as being influential to high-risk perceivers but negative word of mouth discourages purchases. Dissatisfied customers more likely to distribute information through more informal channels. For Flanagin et al., (2014), face-to-face communication is highly effective in changing a consumer product of an opinion, but word of mouth channels can't be relied on when there is a perceived high-risk purchase decision or when there are few formal recommendation channels [139]. However, arguably, with the emergence of digital technologies and social media, there has been a greater dissemination of 'word of mouth,' and information sharing at low cost [140]. Amongst commercial product ratings, if they are too positive people do not find them credible (but only positive and negative) but the average rating of products not necessary quality but where consumers please disappointed. For Myrden and Kelloway (2014) credibility is defined as the customer or clients perceptions that ". . . the firm will do what they are going to do on the next consumption experience with the firm." [141]. Consumer risk (as well as the risk of the seller) is reduced by looking at the ratings of product. Evidence of the volume of ratings as well as a valance, an assessment of product quality can help to ensure product validity and customer satisfaction [142].

As both communication and information sharing technologies have proliferated, determining credible sources has become more complex. In a networked digital media, there is increased disintermediation between information sources and consumers without aid of guidance but an enhanced need to evaluate and assess source information in a variety of contexts [143]. The credibility of an information source is no longer necessarily a feature of face-to-face interaction but established through indirect endorsement but it remains a central component of persuasion for consumer choices [144]. Established information channels may predate the internet such as television (TV) books, magazines, newspapers, and radio, but people perceive credibility differently across variety of information sources. Popular concepts of genres where credibility is paramount are health, news, and reference sources. The role of media credibility is underscored by its function as either a recorder of events or an influencer of opinions [145]. Thus, it influences what people think about and what they think about particular subjects (first and second–level agenda setting). The influence of the media on someone will thus depend on the content of messages and the belief in the credibility of the media [146].

CONSUMER CREDIBILITY

Consumer credibility is based on whether a consumer perceives that claims about a brand or product are truthful. As Oberrmiller et al., (2012) points out, in the helping professions, credibility is understood as having three parts of (perceptions of) competence, character and caring. Perceived competence is disciplinary expertise; professional integrity is perceived character, and empathy and responsiveness is perceived caring [147]. For teachers, those behaviours with the greatest influence on credibility are the purpose, style and accuracy of verbal communications but non-verbal cues, such as body language also have an effect. As Sabri and Geraldine (2014) point out, brand commitment refers to the psychological attachment that customers may have to a brand in a product category [148]. However, consumers tend to reject communication that does not support their position and select information that reinforces their choice. Customers may fend off negative information by developing pro-brand sentiments or waging counter-arguments that detract from negative publicity [149]. Product ratings are used as a barometer of quality, a higher quality is associated with purchasing intentions [150]. Within a reduced cues environment, in which ecommerce takes place, they may mitigate risk [151]. However, often people do not focus on ratings provided, there are cognitive heuristics or short cuts employed, and credibility checks are deemed irrelevant or overridden by consumer desire. Moreover, the task of evaluating all the information on the internet is overwhelming, if not now impossible because of its constant updating and expansion, or at least impossible to the individual person without vast computational aid [152]. When there are obvious cues of information, people employ central processing, but when the information supply is low and trustworthiness harder to determine, then people use peripheral systems or heuristics. However, most time people find online ecommerce to be credible [153].

Sabri and Geraldine also point out that negative stimuli has substantial attention-grabbing power as negative information requires more cognitive effort than positive information [154]. Lachapelle et al., (2014) ask under what conditions does public interpret scientific knowledge claims as credible? In addition, trustworthy? The way experts frame issues and on congruity/dissonance between communication frames [155]. The general public or rational citizens have little incentive their limited time to learn all about the complex issues they face, rather rely on agents with legitimate claim (Downs 1957). People rely on heuristics such as resource cues and value predispositions that act as mental short cuts to assist individuals in forming opinions [156]. Source cues depend on perceptions of source credibility, when given new information decode whether credible so perceptions of source play a role in likelihood of being persuaded [157]. However, they also point out that public trust in scientific evidence and expertise is high, particularly in complex, technical and non-moral issue domains. However, this is tempered by the fact that scientist often disagree and provide member of the public with ‘interpretative flexibility’ [158]. However, when experts disagree people rely on their own predispositions and ‘framing’ (what context they place a judgment in) so holistic attitudes effect perceptions of credibility [159]. Underlying values can lead to bias evaluations and risk can affect evaluations thus experts persuasiveness relies on trustworthiness and expertise.

Others influence people to a greater or lesser extent through a sort of informal social influence. Moreover there is a tendency to ‘accept information obtained from another as evidence about reality,’ and this is a compelling form of persuasion through a process of socio-cognitive normalisation or ‘conversation’ [160]. In the business context, a disgruntled consumer only affects a product’s sales when the product has a small number of ratings but it has a lesser impact over a larger number of negative ratings. Sabri and Geraldine argue that in areas of perceived conflict, evaluators need to disentangle the source cue (such as social status) from the information cue (the framing of the message). In the early stage of opinion formation, individuals rely on prior beliefs more than on cues even when there is information challenging these beliefs [161]. An expert whose message challenges the worldview of others does not enjoy same credibility as another whose message conforms to those dispositions [162]. If an expert frames an issue as low risk those in the public who share an egalitarian worldview may perceive them as less credible, because if there is low dissonance with their own view they cannot be said to have acquired special knowledge. In this circumstance, people will not assign credibility only on credentials, but their message evaluation will relate to the quality of the discourse and the level of perceived cultural bias within it. Hence, people become message evaluators [163].

There are two types of social capital – bridging and bonding social capital. Bridging social capital provides loose social connections that provides access to new information and resources and bonding social capital as about forming strong trusting relationships among people. Word of mouth is still influential and is an increasing phenomenon of the internet. As Jin and Phua (2014) relate, "eWOM refers to "any positive or negative statement made by potential, actual, or former customers about a product or company, which is made available to a multitude of people and institutions via the internet' [164]. Thus product recommendations and ratings have the status equivalent of word of mouth, yet they are semi-permanent and asynchronous (can be accessed at any time).

Grasse et al., (2014) argue that credibility operates like trust as a kind of social 'bank account', it is built up over time through deposits in the form of keeping good practice and commitments [165] However, withdrawals in the form of negative reinforcing actions can be costly to leaders, who attempt to build accounts in the form of employee commitments. Credible leaders challenge processes, search for opportunities, experiment and take risks, envision, and inspire confidence in others. Leaders are often enablers; they foster trust and strength in others, by modelling the way and planning small wins. Leaders need to also demonstrate emotional confidence, including self-awareness [166]. However, self-ratings of behaviours tended to be inflated, invalid, biased, and inaccurate compared with criteria that are more objective.

For Jensen (2013), the range of a communicator's persuasion techniques is called their 'bandwidth.' [167]. If part of the semantic content falls outside the sender's bandwidth, then it will engender a state of expectancy violation. There is a positive increase in credibility when an expected behaviour is better and when negatively evaluated sources conform more closely than expected to cultural values and societal norms. Negative violations of 'bandwidth' over behaviours such as aggression may undermine the credibility of the communicator, and limit the persuasiveness of the communication [168]. Expectations of review narratives if violated may undermine their credibility in three ways. These are lexical complexity, two-sidedness and affect intensity [169]. Lexical complexity involves a higher amount of technical terms and longer words. With two-sidedness a reviewer illustrates both the positive and negative aspects of a product. Marketing campaigns bombard messages, which attempt to cast a product in a positive or negative light. In this situation, a small amount of negative information will increase the probability that a review will be cognitively processed. As Jensen (2013) explains, a small amount of negative information positively violates the expectations of reviewers [170]. Affect intensity refers to the amount of emotional content or emotion-laden words there are in a view, which in turn indicate how strongly the reviewer holds a view [171]. For Fogg et al., (2001) there are seven factors for online credibility: Firstly, 'real world' feel; secondly, ease of use; thirdly, expertise; fourthly, trustworthiness; fifthly, tailoring; sixthly, commercial implications; and seventhly, amateurism, which can involve both 'familiarity' but also incompleteness [172]. However, for Kaur and Dubey (2014), there are two dimensions – expertise and trustworthiness. Expertise is the extent to which a speaker is perceived to be capable of correct assertion; trustworthiness is the degree to which an audience perceives an assertion made by a communicator to be one that the speaker considers valid [173].

As Nagle, Brodsky and Weeter (2014) observe, jurors have a tendency to attend to source-mediated impressions more than content mediated impressions [174]. Rather than use a lot of cognitive effort to process testimony, jurors rely on simple cues such as attractiveness, believability, age, ethnicity, gender and number of arguments. However, jurors do not focus on content when the testimony complex. Facial expressions such as smiling governed by tacit rules indicate a range of emotions. Because of role socialisation, women tend to exhibit more smiling behaviours than men do. Smiling male witness may lose credibility men not expected to smile, may violate gender role by doing so, smiling form women more acceptable than men, women perceived as more likeable, more positive responses to women [175]. Facets of witness credibility include – likeability, confidence, trustworthiness and knowledge. In courtroom attractive dependants less culpable, found guilty less often given more leniency. Absence of smiling and physical attractiveness associated with higher rates of culpability and punishment [176].

Hur, Kim and Woo (2014) studies the relationships amongst corporate social responsibility, corporate brand credibility, equity and corporate reputations. Corporate Social responsibility (CSR) has a positive effect on brand credibility [177]. Consumer willingness is driven sixty-percent by perceptions of company, and forty-percent by perceptions of products. For forty-two percent of people believe that company evaluation is driven by Corporate Social Responsibility (CSR) engagement [178]. When people believe that Corporate Social Responsibility (CSR) stems from sincere behaviour they tend trust a company [179]. In this context a 'service guarantee' "acts as a signal or cue of the anticipated quality of the recovery effort" [180]. Service guarantees may be explicit (specific and in writing) or implicit (an understanding that customer satisfaction will be ensured). This in turn may lead to repurchase intent. For Hur, Kim and Woo (2014) brand equity refers to total utility or value added to a product by virtue of the brand, it is derived from 'fulfilment of consumer expectations' [181]. Corporate reputation is the most important resource providing competitive sustainable advantage that is difficult to create or imitate. Activity is based on human and moral capital (and sometimes potential), which in turn becomes brand credibility. Reputational capital is the consequence of the evaluation of the company, the 'stock' of its 'quality of regard' by stakeholders and clients.

Chapter 5

'In the Zone': Ethics and Relationships

'Next to doing the right thing, the most important thing is to let people know you are doing the right thing' – John D. Rockefeller

Public Relations as a two or many way dialogical relationship between client and stakeholders and the public is all about recognition. If you are familiar with the construct, 'I've seen that symbol somewhere else before . . .!' public relations attempts to close the gap between cognitions and recognitions; or even to inspire like brand management the immediate association between brands, images and beliefs. Nevertheless, if we look at the concept of recognition more deeply it is essential in human social life. It is also critical in the workplace as one of the central communication activities that provides social cohesion, meaning and direction amongst clients *and* staff. Without forms of recognition both formal and informal, high-context and low-context, social and structural, from a simple greeting to an affirmation for competent achievement, the workplace and the human behavior in it may become less than optimal and even dysfunctional. Public Relations is often about recognizing what is best in others – other people, organizations, brands, entities and Public Relations communicators attempt to persuade audiences to recognize positive aspects about the clients they are representing – to see things in their 'best light'.

Businesses advertise to promote their services and to gain clients. Some do so on the basis of the attraction of the goods they offer; others on the skill of the services they provide. To ensure they keep their custom, most business aim to treat their clients politely and with respect. Affirmation and social support are essential for the internal communication in an organization and both stem from the same fundamental communication source – recognition. Employees usually desire to be accepted and everyone likes to be told that they are doing well or doing a good job [181]. However, the unfortunate truth is that many organizational cultures (through lack or professional training or engagement) default to 'deficit' models of communication, in which employees are more often told what they are doing wrong, rather than what they are doing right. Because of the hectic pace of day-to-day business, or because they are more often than not dealing with problem areas, organizations and managers forget to recognize employees. However, as Olson (2008) argues recognition when it is sincere and appreciative goes a long way to reward employees and to promote organizational cohesion [182]. Positive recognition can take many forms, from a one end of the spectrum, simply acknowledging another person through a facial expression, to being socially consistent, voicing a friendly greeting, giving praise, personal thanks, and for an employer giving job recognition such as a raise. Management is about recognizing those who need help but also about praising those who are excelling. For any employee or colleague, paying attention to another person, elaborating on what did well, taking an interest in families without meddling and respecting privacy are all traits of positive recognition in the workplace that go a long way to enhancing organizational culture and producing optimal performance amongst staff.

A professional communicator does not promote statements that are harmful (except disclosure in investment markets). Whereas an ethical communicator is concerned with telling the truth, an unethical communicator does not promote falsehoods but is unconcerned as to whether a statement is true or not [183]. There are five facets to media relations: corporate media relations, articles about the corporation as whole, media relations (stories featuring individual products), marketing Public Relations (coverage of company, products, issues and people) and financial media relations. Each has a distinct function [184]. The press does not have a right to know certain items of kinds of information – proprietary information, personal information, information that is not fully developed or information that would threaten security [185]. So a Public Relations practitioner needs to be mindful of 'what he or she doesn't say, sometimes, as much as what he or she does say.' Furthermore, Public Relations is of course ethically distinct from propaganda which the distortion of truth or the focus on a contextually disengaged proposition for the benefit of an organisation or entity in a one-way communication message. Relatedly, it is also important to distinguish scientific facts (which are independently verifiable and have a transcendental truth-value) from political facts which may accord with the majority point of view independently of its truth-value (for example at one most people believed the world to be flat rather than hemispherical). The executive power of government sometimes rests on political fact and most would believe that it would rarely act against scientific fact but occasionally it might through ommission. So called 'fake news' is not concerned with a 'fact' per se but rather the propagandist is perceived as being the triumphant party or the more believable, in a situation where there are conflicting views. As Michael Leunig noted: "[I]n contemporary art culture, where good looks and clever strategic planning of art careers have become a feature, professional practice may be taught in art schools like a branch of Public Relations or political science."

A company in compliance with laws and regulations also concerns Public Relations with both positive and negative disclosure (the 'reach' or distribution of information. In most corporate or professional contexts, disclosure relates to whether information should be released [186]. One aspect of Public Relations is reputation. Rumour or 'grape-vine' communication is defined as importance multiplied by ambiguity [187]. It is possible to arrive at an approximate formula of reputation as being the sum of constituency images, plus performance and behaviour, plus communication [188]. This occurs in the representation of a company or entity to its constituency or market. It thus follows that a local event may take place in a globalised medium.

As Nelson (2003) argues many companies talk recognition but a 'culture of recognition' is hard to establish. In any organization, employees are the most important source. Some believe that recognition is a human right and for an organization to work well everyone must believe that recognition has a positive impact on employee morale, tenure, performance and productivity [189]. Unfortunately, many organizations do not 'do' recognition well because it is seen as not an intrinsically self-centered activity although it is highly advantageous for organizational purposes. Companies and organizations that do recognize the achievements of their staff well have recognition as an integral part of their culture. As such in large organizations it may be mentioned in value statements, and a part of strategic personnel plans, and an expectation of management – organization shave to work continually to keep recognition 'alive' in the minds of employees [190]. When a culture of recognition is dysfunctional, recognition is perceived of as inequity or favoritism, or worst nepotism.

RECOGNITION AT WORK

One way of improving recognition schemes in the workplace is to ask questions about the way in which recognition is measured and managed. What are the business conditions in which recognition schemes are most often used? Is the practice bottom-up or top-down driven? Are recognition schemes values driven and centrally orientated? Are recognition schemes formal or informal, how is meaning shared amongst them. How does an employ know that there is a correlation between recognition, motivation, increased performance and compensation? In the contemporary workplace, there is a trend towards variable compensation scheme systems, flexible working arrangements, and telecommuting. Most managers agree that recognition of employees enhances performance, that recognition schemes involve staff in providing practical feedback, that it may enable good work to be done, and that some forms of recognition may enhance personal goals of employees. Most people concur that recognition is most effective when it made soon after the causing event or assessment rather than later from it. The incidence of recognition schemes in the workplace is reasonably high but it may not be ingrained in many management practices. As Li, N., Harris, T. B., Zheng, X., Liu, X. (2016) state, recent estimates – three out of four organizations use formal recognition programs [191]. Such systems primarily involve non-financial, symbolic gestures of appreciation, which have incentive types tailored to individual preference [192]. Li, et al., note that it is possible that ". . . formally identifying and recognizing a top performer may boost other teammates' productivity via key social influence processes. . .' [193]. However, competition can sometimes provide negative stimulus for those who are unsuccessful in gaining the reward of recognition. Social influence has a powerful effect on recognition levels within an organization. Both role modelling recognition and social learning of recognition behavioral repertoires and responses can produce a positive spillover effect in which a performer who is recognized formally may enhance a recipient teammates' individual and collective performance [194]. When there is an economy of exchange along recognition behavior dimensions within an organization, and formal recognition of individuals and team's recognition programs may boost performance and morale and produce positive spillover effects. Such recognition events are also acknowledgement of organizational values and messages of affirmation and reinforcement [195]. So too with acknowledging mistakes, better to be frank and open, than withdrawing – do it quickly, for as Henry Kissinger once put it: "[i]f it's going to come out eventually, better have it come out immediately."

A defining attribute of self-other relations is relatedness which brings people together in behaviors that involve recognition of one-another. As such, it seen, that recognition occurs in both an 'intimate sphere' of individuals and 'public sphere' of groups and politics. Although the sense it is employed in most organizations belongs to an individuated sense of a collective identity, as a system of reward it is often focused primarily at individual level, although how national, ethnic groups are viewed or valued becomes a cumulative factor of culturally embedded recognition behaviors [196].

Recognition of oneself (through reflective practices) and recognition of others through reflective practices is related to behaviors of respect though it is conceptually distinct because it is based in inherent human values that are grounded in notions of dignity. All human interactions affect ideas and perceptions of dignity. Positive self-other relations in which positive other regard is received is understood to increase a person's sense of dignity. By comparison, a negative recognition decreases human dignity.

Given that most people within organizations are embedded in complex social systems, which have reciprocal influences, incentive in the form of recognition may improve positive normalizing functions. In this context it is relevant to note that social influence is seen as a process of information sharing and leaning in which employees selectively determine informational relevance and can assign behavioral utility to others. Recognition schemes may provide strong tangible signals to others in valuing behaviors and conferring legitimating roles on recipients [197]. Recognition is on a spectrum of formality or informality. As Li et al. (2016) note, people constantly make active and passive observation of others, and at times people make vicarious assessments of others as a part of ordinary behavior. Social ties permit or prohibits the observation of others, network patterns, and the proximity of neighbors and in group and out-group behaviors [198]. The centrality of people within the network of workflow amplifies the positive effect of recognition on team performance, which also influences those on the periphery [199].

Peer Recognition Schemes

Of the various recognition methods, peer recognition has a powerful effect on staff morale and motivation. Recognition is meaningful when it comes from colleagues and schemes that are based on the idea that staff can nominate their colleagues for a reward and management can decide from the nominations which is more deserving are not costly in terms of resources and promote good communication and motivation. Such peer recognition schemes promote organizational values and responsibility. If peer recognition schemes are linked to business objectives and avoid being popularity contests, they are more effective [200]. Some peer recognition schemes are based on revenue and targets, they are cross-functional and collaborative, and some give employees a choice of reward. Although receiving an award from peer nomination can boost morale, not everyone thrives on being in the limelight [201].

Recognition as a Form of Social Capital, the 'Building Blocks' of PR

Aldrich notes that 'social capital' namely the 'networks, norms, and social trust that facilitate coordination and cooperation for 'mutual benefit'. As Ross and Carter (2011) explain, "[t]he spontaneous activation of 'social capital' – bonds within and between social groups – [is] impressive, a solace to those affected, as well as a huge practical and economic benefit." [202]. 'Human capital' is the ability of people to remain co-operative and resilient in communities and to work in a co-ordinated way together on issues in common. Social capital is an enabler of trust and like human recognition is relational, involving interactions among individuals and groups [203]. Public Relations practitioners aim to activate and strengthen for of social capital through networking with stakeholders. Obviously, Public Relations practitioners do so in order to raise and improve the profile of the organization or person on behalf of whom they are acting, Public Relations is thus mainly about promotion of an organization, its brand and thus its business capabilities. However, the recognition that is involved in strengthening organizational profile through contact with stakeholders also has a psychological dimension. Dimensions of recognition are both material and psychological and can directly and indirectly influence well-being [204]. In terms of psychological effects, the level and quality of human recognition that is received by a person directly affects their well-being, independently of material outcomes [205]. A person who is acknowledged and recognized by others is more likely to feel 'in-tune' with the environment, and more likely to be both connected and harmonized. A person who is ignored is more likely to retreat socially, to be less self-expressive and to feel out of tune with the environment. He or she is less likely to seek reciprocal interaction and may be more prone to self-regulative thoughts. Such psychological effects of recognition or its absence can have real 'material effects' on behaviors and actions for example which in turn affect other outcomes such as health, status, income and education. Given that there is a subtle but tangible effect that the level of recognition can have on the actions and behaviors of both the individual providing recognition and the material well-being of the person who receives the recognition, then there is a behavioral causal relationship between other-regarding 'healthy' and 'less healthy' behaviors [206]. Furthermore, these impacts are sometimes expressed through behavioral access towards opportunities and services. Social recognition may have both individual factors and a shared value horizon and common standard of judgment but make individual differences socially visible [207].

From a Public Relations perspective, organizations, which are attractive or prestigious, are more likely to foster seducement to enhance person's self-esteem but this self-esteem may be derived from an external source [208]. As any form of identity forming process, recognition may produce both enhanced (when positive) and degraded affect (when negative) and often variations between [209]. Understanding the possibilities of social capital through recognition schemes, rebranding, stakeholder liaison, marketing and promotion of an organization or person, is crucial to the Public Relations practitioner. Sometimes expectations of recognition are met and sometimes they are not. Arguably, highly inviting monetary rewards may be insufficient for producing positive relation to self over time because most involve some sacrifice to some notions of self in process [210]. Establishing 'ethical moments' emerging relation-to-self address position in world such as in conferral or withholding of recognition is on a continuum of agonizing and emotional experiences [211]. A way of mitigating this issue is for employees to ensure congenial working conditions and for improving material development outcomes involving higher levels of recognition. A mutuality results. Individuals who receive higher levels of positive recognition are more likely to provide positive recognition to others; those that receive lower levels of recognition are likely to provide similar levels to others [212]. Honneth (1996) regards recognition as firstly, positive affirmation of a person's characteristics; secondly, an attitude realized in concrete action; and thirdly, distinct phenomenon of social world – the result of side effect of an action [213]. However, there are differences between forms of recognition and levels of both affect and perception. For example, 'love' may be a form of mutual care and affection and 'formalized' in a relationship of 'cognitive – rational' effect between legally equal partners. It may be distinguished from legal recognition, in which subjects are autonomous and morally responsible, and distinguished from rights-based recognitions derived from legal status and charters.

Employers and employees are in a relationship of agency and responsibility. As Fassauer and Hartz (2016) argue, "various instances of agency" aim to affect an organizational order [214]. As Sandberg and Kubiak (2013) relate, in many workplaces recognition is expressed through "tangible affordances of engagement" in participatory practices, work tasks, opportunities for decision-making [215]. Three varieties of misrecognition occur. Firstly, resistance, either an individual or colleagues do not identify them with recognition, or the available recognition schemes are unaligned with aspirations and personal appraisal of learning; secondly, marginalization whereby and individual's aspirations are not recognizable within setting's participatory opportunities; and, thirdly, rejection whereby, participatory opportunities incompatible with individual's capabilities, experience of or active mutual rejection of possible anticipation [216].

As Ledingham and Bruning (1998) state Public Relations involves relationship management [217]. Organisations with service need to keep in mind that there are several variables and valences that determine whether a customer is happy, undecided or even whether they will switch to someone new. These valences are: trust, openness, involvement, investment and commitment. If the company establishes a relationship with these factors then it is ahead in the sphere of relationship management. Relationships are central to Public Relations, as it is a field, which aims to maintain mutually beneficial relationships between an organisation and its publics on whom success depends and view Public Relations as relationship management [218]. Public Relations involves a conceptual change, it blends the relationship management function with a communication activity. There are both symmetrical and asymmetrical models of relationships that involve mutual benefit for an organisation. Not just symbolic activity but long-term behavioural relationships between clients, organisations and their key publics (56) [219].

According to Brunner (2008), a relational dialectics involve dimensions of commitment, trust and comfort. Trust refers to the feeling that people can rely on each other and it is predicated on dependability and forthrightness [220]. The dialectics show the tensions of engagement in the relationship between autonomy and connection, novelty and predictability, openness and closedness. Other factors to consider are the extent to which mutual goals are aligned, the extent to which there is a power imbalance, the extent to which there is a comparison of levels of alternatives, shared technology and or social bonds.

For Gombita, relationship building involves connections, informal and informal, short or long term that have developed with various stakeholders [221]. A stakeholder is a person or organization with an interest or concern to be involved in the activities of the client and or organisation. In any positive relationship, building activity there is a bond, liaison, link, tie, or union. Most elements pertain to personal and informal connections, which are publicised or realised in social media and become part of networking and engagement practices.

Organisations relate to one-another by participating on various platforms, with integrated communication strategies, and advisers, tacticians or practitioners demonstrate knowledge and skills in making use of channels, with as needs be, both accountability and creativity! Yet, as Boie states the relationships between an organisation and its publics representations (clients, stakeholders, primary and secondary audiences), are traditionally of function of the management uses of strategic communication [222]. Changing attitudes and behaviours part-and-parcel of what Public Relations practitioners do but changing perceptions is not easy. According to Suster, the best ways of improving relationships with journalists involve:

- Good product knowledge
- Treating as human
- Understand their needs
- Help them better do their job
- Getting a fair shot
- Fighting back fairly [223].

Measuring Relationships in Public Relations

Public relations practitioners closely monitor the outcome of their stakeholder and / or media engagement. They aim to measure, (by a raft of 'tools' such as survey' and opinion poll) changes before and after intervention of the implementation of communication plans. They measure what is present and how well an organisation presents itself to others, the amount of attention and exposure it receives, and they measure whether target audiences have received the messages directed at them and responded to and paid attention to them – whether they have understood them, and retained them [224]. Public Relations practitioners might hope to achieve mutuality which is understood as the degree to which parties agree on who has rightful power to influence one another. Similarly, trust involves a party's level of confidence and willingness to open oneself to another party. There are many dimensions to organisational trust [225]:

- Integrity -- a belief that the organisation is just and fair
- Dependability -- the belief that the organisation will do what it says it will do

- Competence – the belief that the organisation has the ability to fulfil its mission.
- Satisfaction – extent to which party feels favourably toward positive expectations about relationship reinforced.
- Commitment – relationship worth spending energy to maintain, promote.

There are (generally) two types of business relationships: Firstly, exchange relationships in which one party benefits the other because of reciprocal future expectation; and secondly communal relationships in which there are mutually shared goals. The Public Relations communication plan will determine whether messages are being sent, attended to in press releases, what kind of publications are issued, where they are placed in the media. What sort of media monitoring will be done, what outcomes and changes in cognitions, attitudes and behaviour of the publics are desirable. However, the effects of Public Relations are not easily measured, whether or not the objectives are achieved, we cannot measure the totality of the value easily [226]. One evaluative measure frequently adopted in environmental scanning, which looks for positive or negative feedback about the organisation from the environment. It is revealed that organisations are better able to achieve their goals when the internal and external values and goals are aligned. Furthermore, organisations make better decisions when they listen to and collaborate with stakeholders. Changes in relationships affect changes in the publics' behaviour. Arguably, the development of long-term relationships are better as they avoid conflict, litigation, complains and get less interference from government. As Doorley and Garcia (2015) state: "[r]ecognizing the relationship between ethical lapses and reputational harm, many companies now see commitment to ethics as an integral part of managing their relationship and preserving the value of the company's intangible assets." [227]. These are made when organisations plan, implement and evaluate relationships with key stakeholders and publics. An organisation's public orientation may occupy any one of a number of positions, they may be integrative, distributive, asymmetrical and of dual concern. Other relationships may be those of trust, satisfaction and commitment [228]; and or communal relationships [229]. Organisations may be contending (an organisation tries to convince a public to accept a position); it may be avoiding (it may leave a market or context of conflict psychologically or physically); it may be accommodating whereby the organisation yields, in part, and lowers its aspirations; or it may be compromising by cooperating or becoming unconditionally constructive. There is a sense of reciprocity requires in which the organisation counts suggestions, complaints, inquiries or other interactions from staff. Other measurements of the efficacy of Public Relations advisers may include the frequency with which management seeks them out for advice willing to disclose intentions, decisions, and behaviours. There are three main strata to organisational Public Relations:

- Media relations
- Employee relations
- Marketing communications

Public Relations as Bowen states, aims to be inclusive of values such as honesty, openness, loyalty, fair-mindedness, respect, integrity and forthrightness. Public Relations can be an ethical practice but traditionally it has been seen as unethical in some contexts leading to use of terms such as with 'spin doctoring,' 'faction', prpoaganda and even espionage. However, good Public Relations *disentangles* propaganda and media manipulation it does not propagate it. Although people may claim that the media attempts to deliberately obfuscate, deceive and derail public debate, the main effort of Public Relations is to respond effectively to these mediated challenges. In some circles there is a perception that Public Relations practitioners are invisible people controlling public debate and public opinion, twisting reality and protecting the powerful from any negative press. The early days of media engagement emphasised hyperbole, sensationalism, and a lack of truth -- Ivy Lee's[1] adage – 'the public be damned!'. Yet socially responsible corporate policy has far-reaching effects, as does its neglect. It can be default inspire or inhibit civil unrest, promote or demote the call for government and businesses to higher levels of accountability such as those found with tiple-bottom-line reporting. Arguably, it is a function of reputation managers to advise executives on ethically responsible policy. But traditionally not all public relations strategists automatically have the ear of those in power – though increasingly this may be changing. It is standard in today's business world for approximately 65% of Public Relations practitioners to report to the CEO, of their client organisation and for the remaining 35% to report at executive level [230]. Hence practitioners need to be conversant with issues of risk and crisis management, leadership, organisational culture, policy and ethics.

Dialogue is the basis of Public Relations and involves the chance for all interested parties have input, in an open engagement in which they judged on their merits until truth comes out. It is the good character of the organisation to communicate with its publics, to discuss the organisation and issues with stakeholders in an 'ongoing' dialogue of give and take – a 'two way street.' This sometimes involves the Public Relations practitioner in a role similar to an attorney, involving a dialectic of persuasion. Practitioners often aim to produce utilitarian outcomes, which are more long-term goals that integrate what some of publics want. To achieve this management engages in ongoing relationships, in which they are seen as consequences and potential outcomes, and in which ethical decisions are defined as those, which maximise positive consequences. Guideline behaviours include:

- Knowing organisational or client values
- Issues management
- Knowing the organisational culture
- Educating decision makers

[1] Ivy Ledbetter Lee (1877 – 1934) was the founder of contemporary public relations, which he used as a noun in the preface of the 1897 *Yearbook of Railway Literature*.

- Analysing ethical dilemmas
- Recognising that no-one person has an entire ethical conscience.

Role Conflict and Ambiguity

Ethics transgressions and violations can sometimes lead to retributions towards others or towards the organisation. This may simply take the form of a complaint against policy or procedure, inter-personal conflict, or even mediation and legal dispute resolution. The two central components of ethical failure include the origin of a particular offense and whether an organisation or an institution commits it. The seriousness of the ethical failure is determined by three subcomponents: Firstly, whether the ethical failure was a first time occurrence; secondly, what the type of offense was; thirdly, the impact or seriousness of the offense, and fourthly, how widespread was the occurrence? [231]. Crises will vary from being minor to major in magnitude.

In the context of the creation of ethically compliant environments it is not necessarily the case that 'getting the science right' overrides all other considerations in an organisational context, not to say that it is wrong, but rather that the deontological approach (or organisational conduct) must also be valid and preferably stable and consistent [232]. Argyis et al., (1985) stated that organisational effectiveness is higher in circumstances where there is a congruence between the espoused organizational values and actual organisational practices [233]. In some circumstances 'clan' cultures (or groups of like-minded people that share inter-personal or collegiate alliances) can be stronger and more effective than bureaucratic cultures [234]. Sometimes, however in business environments, the individual who excels is not necessarily valued highly as a team member [235]. Fortunately, many organisational environments can sustain both team-members and those who work best as individuals may reward both styles equally.

Ethics failure is defined as being a "result of a sustained period of value conflict or dissonance usually resulting in frustration, anger and perhaps isolation of the part of a casualty member in (his or) her attempt to achieve recognition for reaching institutional goals for one's work" [236]. Consequently, not all-unethical behaviour is motivated by deficiency in values but rather in conflict or dissonance in behavioural or procedural expectations. A solution for value dissonance is simply better management of diverse cultures in academia by administrative gatekeepers of cultures) [237]. Bruhn argues that value dissonance can be avoided by: Firstly, greater proactive management of institutions' cultures beginning with the socialisation of new faculty; secondly, annual monitoring of individual faculty member's progress in meeting institutional norms; thirdly, increasing opportunities and rewards for faculty to engage in collaborative process across disciplinary boundaries. This may lessen the possibility of faculty isolation and discontent when they encounter disappointment or frustration [238]. Siloism, which means the creation of an organisation microclimate of intellectual isolationism, can be caused by many factors – resistance to change, poor communication, or intransigence on a particular process or issue.

As Gower (2006) notes Public Relations also has an emphasis on transparency, or 'what you see is what you get'. Demand for increased visibility based on assumptions that may not be true will not be effective but consumers for most part are only interested in assurances of proper hehaviour [239]. But in most interactions with clients and organisations, the public stakeholder does not have unlimited information. Critics argue that public is not really interested in *everything* that people, organisations and corporations are disclosing, however, often a little amount of information disclosure goes a long way!. Usually more information leads to greater trust and credibility, however, information per se is not the same thing as transparency of or trust. Organisations can use transparency to obscure reality, to hide rather than reveal, while this may not constitute mis-direction, it is certainly a form of magic trick! To get the message across to the client, stakeholders and audiences, Public Relations practitioners generally have specific goals in mind:

- Counteracting negative publicity
- Making a client's viewpoint known
- Ensuring balanced media coverage
- Helping media and public understand complex issues
- Defusing hostile environment
- Resolving conflict.

According to Mersham, Theunissen and Peart (2009), Public Relations practitioners are constantly engaged in issues management, which involves identifying, monitoring and analysing trends in public opinion, which could create future problems for an organisation. In addition, when they are pro-active in their messaging and publicity they are trendsetters [240].

Chapter 6

'HEY, WHOSE SIDE ARE YOU ON ANYWAY?': ADVOCACY AND PERSUASION

'Advertising is saying you're good. PR is getting someone else to say you're good' -- Jean-Louis Gassee

Mental gymnastics. Have you ever played the game 5 X 5? You are given a five word or less scenario such as 'Profits are down, competition is up'. 'In groups of five you have five seconds to each think of a reason to persuade another group why they should support the business. Often the first thought that comes to mind is the best. Like being an advocate, the Public Relations strategist's role is 'mental gymnastics.' In the quickest time in the most efficient way, how do you best represent the goals and intentions of your client? Public Relations and reputation management, as forms of mental gymnastics, require adept uses of language.

Language is a medium of social exchange; it is the primary locus of meaning in the everyday world, the central method by which people communicate, barring non-verbal communication which arguably is interpretd if not symbolically structured by language-based thought. Language can be seen as a bridging device between two spaces – that of concepts and ideas and also the articulation and communication of those concepts. Bridging spaces is essential to Public Relations practice as a dialogic activity between two or more parties, client and stakeholder. So when considering language it is useful to think of how it is 'made-up' what are the 'nuts and bolts' of language use? Linguists will tell us that there are generally understood to be five main branches of rhetorical comprehension in language, these are [241]: Firstly, phonetics which is the production and perception of sounds or manual gestures, secondly, phonology which is the systematic behaviour of languages sounds; thirdly, morphosyntax which is a system that combines meaningful units of sound into sentences and words, fourthly, semantics which is the study of word meanings, and fifthly, pragmatics which is a system for relating word meaning to the communicative intention of speaker or writer. The purpose of written communication is first to relay information to the reader. Secondarily, it is to relate that information to the reader in a particular way – to persuade the reader of a particular point of view. Persuading people of a particular point of view is a core Public Relations strategy. The art and science of written persuasion is the provenance of rhetoric which is both the 'how' and 'why' of written communication, and indeed of the rhetoric of persuasion within Public Relations.

Although having origins in the first millennia of Christian Europe, from an historical perspective the rise of rhetorical composition was coeval with the spread of literacy following the invention of the mechanical printing press. It was fuelled by tensions between church and state, legal progress and reform, the expansion of commerce (and records and writing to service it). All these led to conditions under which rhetorical composition and letter writing was deemed useful and necessary. The waning of papal influence and the growth of secular government and the spread of forms of commerce such as property ownership conjointly with the spread of literacy mean that the *ars dictaminis* assumed an important place in the functioning of medieval society [242]. The art of composition writing was developed further in medieval universities and became known as the *dictamen prosaicum or ars distaminis,* and found practical outlet in everyday affairs of life including the recording of official wills, commendations, contracts, immunities and so forth [243]. The composition of rhetorical writing was informed by such factors as choice of diction (elegantia), sentence skill (composition), and the expression of human dignity (dignitas, ornatur) [244]. There were three main kinds of dictamin – prose or free composition, metrical composition (which is an art and science of measures) and rhythmical composition which follows syllabic equality and rime [245]. All of which involved the statement of facts in as clear and simple language as possible, observing qualities of precision, exactitude, and systematic verification and record [246]. Thomas states that the *artes dictandi* was informed by five features of letter writing, these included the asulatation (salutation), the capturing of good will (Catatio Benevolentiae), the statement of facts (narration), the petition for action (petition), and the conclusion [247]. Thomas also notes that rhetorical composition also involved tutorage in style which involved the use of coloribus (translated as 'colors') but might also be related to related to what is called in Public Relations terms 'spin' – or the ability to effect audience perception [248]. This led to the development of the belletrist movement, which posited that rhetoric; letter-writing and imaginative literature could be joined under the heading of 'rhetoric and belles lettres' as a distinct form of composition [249]. The fact that rhetorical composition has endured as an art over literally more than a millennia attests to its enduring function in civilised society.

In most writerly contexts, and in Public Relations compositions, Grice's principle may be at work that is that there is a basic co-operation between writers and readers in the assumption that a text will communicate between them effectively. According to Grice (1989), the cooperative principle is a form of guide to clear communication, he states, "[m]ake your contribution such as it is required, at the stage at which it occurs, by the accepted purpose or direction of the talk exchange in which you are engaged" [250]. Conversational implicature involves four maxims; quantity, quality, relation and manner determine these. Information needs to be given only such as is appropriate to the level of exchange. The lawyer's responsibility not to mislead (or to be false) is asserted along with the concern to make statements without evidence, so too the Public Relations communication consultant has an ethical to represent the client but also to the stakeholder and the public, to represent 'the truth'.

Relevancy is valued as is clarity of expression or at least avoiding obscurity, ambiguity, unnecessary prolixity, and accentuating the orderly. The ambiguity that may be associated with conversational implicature or the ability to say one thing and imply another – for example, humour, bathos, irony etc) is conditioned by a further four factors. These are: nondetachability (or it appears that the same thing could not be said in a different way to bear the same meaning) [251]; secondly, cancelability, either explicitly (for example,. x but not x) or contextually if there is a situation in which the meaning is literal or nonsensical [252]; thirdly, non-conventionality – two meanings may emanate from the same speech act [253]; fourthly, calculability, it must be capable of being understood [254]. Conversational implicatures are redolent is some aspects of everyday social speech – especially the more performative areas in which social relations or human character comes into play – they are those strong features of linguistic humanism, which are conventionally deployed to good effect in rhetorical composition. What this boils down to is to say something that represents reality as clearly as possible and as openly and engagingly as the Public Relations practitioner is able to. As Anita Loos put it: "[t]he rarest of all things in American life is charm. We spend billions every year manufacturing fake charm that goes under the heading of Public Relations. Without it, America would be grim indeed." If money makes the world go round, manners politeness and a good explanation can also go a long way.

Confirming the hypothesis that the style of rhetoric is driven by 'factors of four,' James argues that the main determinations of rhetorical composition (that towards which the writer argues) are issues of fact (the dispute or restitution about what is objectively known, issues of definition (what counts as a thing rather than another thing), issues of quality (what is the composition of thing and how does it relate to us as a concept of instrumental or even aesthetic utility), and issues of process (how does a thing do the thing that it does) [255]. Furthermore, most rhetorical compositions have a quadruple structure determined by the basic question of a topic or problem (the thing towards which or about which the writer writes), the proof that is required to support or refute the position that is being asserted, the refutation of a counter-factual perspective, and a conclusion which poses a solution or response to the topic and issues [256]. It is also usual to make a claim following the positing of a question, which contains a topic or problem; this claim will assert the overall position or argument of the composition. The topic, question or claim of the composition is then followed by reasons which support a particular point of view that are followed by evidence which either affirms of does not contradict the reasons for the claims so made. It is common practice for rhetorical compositions to also make concessions to a particular point of view (sometimes expressed as 'arguing around a topic') or to demonstrate strong or weak positions for the argument asserted in support of the claims, As well as providing a response or solution to the topic under discussion warranties are sometimes also provided which demonstrate the parameters of validity for the argument – conditions under which the argument may be supported and limits to its efficacy [257]. These are implicit in such aphorisms, as 'the organisation which goes the extra mile'.

The persuasiveness of rhetorical composition may also be judged by five factors. These are sufficiency (how neatly does the topic argument address the topic features); representativeness – how well does the composition represent the structure and argument of the topic; accuracy – how precise is the information provided and how logical or demonstrative is the argument made; relevance – to what extent does the topic question and argument composition strike resonance with its readers, to what extent is the topic one that appeals to or concerns its readers, how meaningful is the context of the discussion?; and finally, an authoritative rhetorical composition needs to demonstrate mastery of a topic area and a degree of persuasiveness that creates a genuine impression on the reader [258].

Thus, elements of persuasive rhetoric in compositional writing (and in Public Relations) share much in common with scientific writing, with business report writing and indeed with the methodology of auditing. In the first, the scientific composition proceeds from hypothesis (the theory or event that the experiment seeks to measure or test), to an outline of the methods employed, to a discussion of findings and results, to conclusions about what is discovered and or the validity and applicability of the outcome. In the second, the scientific or business report there is an identification of the issue, a discussion of the background or context of the study, an explication of the current position and applicability of the report design, next comes the methodological explanation, a discussion of findings and results follows, and lastly advice, commentary and recommendations on the discovery of the report. The audit is by comparison more perfunctory, consisting of an identified issue, the background to the issue, methods of discovery, findings, followed by a conclusion with recommendations. While the rhetorical composition shares structural elements in common with these three common varieties of exposition, it nevertheless contains elements that they may lack. Namely, a factor of persuasion facilitated by reasoned argument that may confirm or refute previous findings in the context of the composition, and significantly an argument, which may conform to humanist principles of, reasoned advocacy.

The overall aim of the rhetorical composition in Public Relations as in other business fields is to produce a balance between authority and readability. The main unit of the construction in the rhetorical composition is the sentence itself of which there are generally thought to be four types. This declarative sentence makes a statement or assertion of a particular fact, set of facts, or point of view. This is often used co-jointly with the interrogative sentence the purpose of which is to ask a question, or to set in course a particular seed of doubt or scepticism in the reader. The imperative sentence in comparison issues a command, a compulsion for a particular event or action to be described. The exclamation sentence is used to express emphasis or to articulate surprise [259].

There are also two factors of sentence writing that may detract from audience appeal. These are 'parallelism,' which involves the use of related pairs within a sentence, or a series of words and phrases, and 'repetition' (which in some circumstances – particularly in oratory may be used to good effect) but which is closely related to parallelism, and can lead to redundancy of information and the deterioration of the reader's interest. In comparison, 'apposition' is a form of emphasis, which provides further details on a particular point of view but commenting on it or qualifying it in some way. Parenthesis may also be used sparingly and to good effect by breaking up the monotony of standard sentences by the insertion of a middle element, which provides further details [260].

One of the central motivations, if not compulsions behind the rhetorical composition is that of either humanist or scientific interest which also bears a tangential responsibility to the concerns of public discourse and truth-telling. As Ebel et al., (2004) state, "[e]verything measured, detected, invented or arrived at theoretically in the name of science must, as soon as possible, be made public . . ." [261]. Thus, the motivations of rhetorical composition are similar to those of science but more than this without the exchange and dissemination of information, science and public discourse could not take place [262].

Thus, central to the Public Relations is communication. As Ebel et al., (2004) states, communication involves the mutual access to information, and "[f]rom a linguist's perspective 'communication' suggests a direct, substantive exchange (interaction), either oral or written, involving two or more distinct parties" [263]. Every writer should write for an audience and as if there is a reader present (however remote this reader is from them in space and time), and even if that reader is only themselves (as in forms of code). The Latin term for information exchange is *communicare* – to have something in common. So central is communication to the scientists of rhetoricians' practice that it is in fact the central activity in which they are engaged.

Public Relations involves any activity that is relationship enhancing, which mediates public disputes and which advocates on behalf of a client or position and which achieves a mutual understanding among parties [264]. At the basis of the need for Public Relations, writing is the fact that once information is uncontrolled it may be at the mercy of the media interests (and thereby come under control of others who may or may not share the point of view taken). By comparison controlled information is the writer's tool – a writer may be influenced by editorial content, style, placement and timing of information [265].

The element that rhetorical composition has in common with Public Relations writing is that of persuasion. Some people regard persuasion of any form (because it is inherently biased) as being unethical. Because most of us living in liberal democracies have some notion of a public and private state (that is, there elements of both public and private contexts in most people's lives). There is also a conjoining (but frequently threatened notion) that either the freedom of ideas and discourse (as in the public sphere) or a 'marketplace of ideas (as in the private sphere) will provide enough confirming, disconfirming or 'different' information (that is unbiased) for people to make up their minds over any one issue. Although ostensibly the political system is based on this theory, it may also be based on a notion of reasoned argument amongst these differing, reinforcing, or contradictory beliefs. No two points of view will be the same and hence one position, that is more reasonably argued, may become more persuasive than another [266]. For the most part unethical techniques could be thought to be conditions of over-persuasiveness or of personal favouritism, or simply (as was believed to be the case in Roman society) of logical fallacies (or mistake or errors) in reasoned argument.

In Public Relations writing, as in other forms of rhetorical composition, there are many techniques and sources of persuasive argument that may be variously considered (or at least be on a continuum of tactical use and thus ethical or unethical consideration. Those that might be considered unethical are: Firstly, 'personal attack' which aims at discrediting the source of the message regardless of the message itself, secondly, the 'bandwagon' effect – which makes an aim for popularity, thirdly, inference by association which is an argument based on false logic, guilt or credit by association, fourthly, the 'plain folks' argument which appeals to a need to deal with people who are like-minded, similar, and 'no-nonsense'; fifthly, testimonials which are inferences by association – for an example the use of a celebrity who endorses a product, sixthly, 'transfer' which is a technique which involves the use of positive symbols to transfer meaning to a message that is not necessarily related [267].

A subset of unethical persuasive argument is that of unethical language use. This may involve equivocation (the notion that words are ambiguous and may have more than one meaning); secondly amphiboly which is ambiguous sentence structure and grammar use which may mislead the reader; thirdly, emotive language which is the use of impassioned or colourful vocabulary which shifts the response from the argument itself to images invoked by words [268]. Conversely, there are five main concepts to be used in ethical persuasion or communicative practice, these are: firstly, to be honest and accurate in communications, secondly, to act promptly to correct erroneous communications for which the practitioner may be responsible, thirdly, to preserve and respect copyright and intellectual property rights; fourthly, to investigate the truthfulness and accuracy of information that is presented either on behalf of oneself or on the behalf of others [269]. When ethical discourse is infringed in a public context it can lead to defamation, which is the word, used to describe the status of any communication, which holds up another to contempt, hatred, ridicule or scorn. Defamation may or may not involve legal remedy. As Bivin's states, there are five factors, which may lead to defamation in any communication. These are:

- A statement which harms the reputation of another
- The message must be communicated or published
- A person defamed must be identified, directly
- The victim so identified must be able to demonstrate harm to reputation
- An act of negligence must be shown on behalf of the communicant [270].

The art of persuasion (when it is considered as a verb) includes the concept of moving someone to believe or act in a certain way – though this is usually thought of as being in the context of mutual understanding given the fact that when people exchange any information there is usually a process of misunderstanding or interpretative difference. However, 'dissonance theory' in Public Relations writing is the name given for the general tendency for people to seek messages that are consonant with their own existing beliefs or attitudes, the fact that people do not seek messages that are different from pre-held existing beliefs [271]. Within Public Relations, writing there exists a perception of publics that are informed by at least four interpretative frameworks. These are selective exposure – the notion that people seek out information that agrees with existing beliefs; selective attention – people tend not to process communication that goes against existing attitudes and pay attention only to self-confirming information; selective perception – people only interpret information that agrees with their attitudes or points of view which either leads to misinterpretation or reinterpretation (and distortion of information; fourthly, the 'elaboration likelihood model' which argues that people are easy to persuade, whereas others are resistant to persuasion, and some who argue about those whose opinions they oppose [272]. However, another view argues that receivers and perceivers of messages either cognate on messages extensively before being persuaded (and thus may amplify or elaborate on a message) or those of cognate less or not at all about received information but may instead rely on an auxiliary range of messages to make decisions but this is derived from an understanding primarily of marketing messaging [273]. Some people have an inherent need for message clarity and disambiguation, whereas others may be more comfortable tolerating higher levels of ambiguity. However, generally speaking personal issues involve a greater amount of cognition. This may be due simply to self-interest, or the difficulty of separating self from relevant issues. In terms of the style of composition, rhetoricians argue for the virtue of such factors as [274]:

- Writing to an absent person as if that person was present
- Writing in a concise manner without being obscure
- Avoiding excessive display and practicing naturalness and ease in letter-writing
- Avoiding ambiguities
- Preserving an open personality
- Preserving clarity, unity and coherence
- Maintaining an open-mindedness towards adaptation
- Maintaining courtesy by adjusting to the reader
- Conveying energy to excite the imagination and arouse feeling

However, Public Relations writing and rhetorical composition writing share in the concern with persuasion that people may be motivated to change their mind based on three factors. These are: Firstly, to what extent are they aware of the issue in general; secondly, to what extent it is important to them personally; and thirdly, whether they believe their own opinion will be influential [275].

The strategies employed in either rhetorical composition or Public Relations may be influenced by a variety of techniques and devices. Above all, it is useful to have a clear understanding of how readers respond and to convey messages in clear terms and with opposing points of view. It is useful to note that in either rhetorical composition or in Public Relations, a persuasive message is frequently audience centered and the strategy is based on who your audience is and how the members of the audience react subjectively to a topic. One aspect that is related to personal bias is 'identification,' the tendency for people to relate to an idea or opinion if they can see some direct effect on their own hopes, fears or aspirations [276]. Frequently also there is an 'agency effect' of ideas – the tendency for people only to endorse a particular point of view if it also entails a proposed action especially an action of expediency. Trust is also an inherent feature persuasion – people are only likely to invest cognitive congruency in people from whom they are willing to accept ideas. There may also be a familiarity effect in which people will discount information from those to whom they do not attribute trust.

Once ideas are asserted and an argument made for a particular position, compliance strategies may be used which are designed to gain agreement through techniques not based on reasoned argument but on other methods such as familiarity or authority. Occasionally 'sanction strategies' (or arguments) may use as rewards or punishments that may arise from a particular situation or controlled by audience members. 'Appeal strategies' may call on an audience to aid a communicator or a party represented by a communicator. Furthermore, command strategies may be used to direct requests but may himself or herself lack rationale or motivation although an accompanying explanation may be given for reasons for complying. Argument strategies are designed to oppose a point of view or to persuade others sometimes these might be compelled by reasoned argument – a motivated sequence, a question and answer session and attitudinal change messages [277].

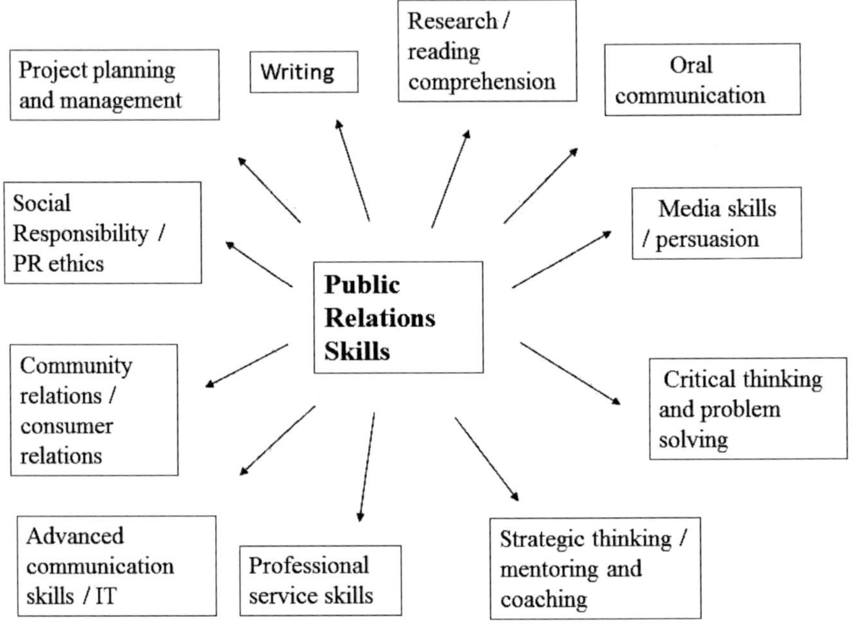

Figure 1. Showing the Public Relations Skillset.

A strategy that is used in devising rhetorical compositions and in Public Relations writing is that of engaging with an audience by writing for the audience and imagining the audience response. The writer asking a series of questions related to the imagined reader can achieve this. These include such basic statements as asking why the subject is important, how and in what way attitudes need changing, what oppositional argument be might be, what is the opposing view? Has it been represented fairly? What is the fundamental position that is asserted and how is it supported? An assessment of whether the audience agrees with your point of view and an assembly of arguments, which may support this position. Techniques, which are used in advertising Public Relations, may also be employed in rhetorical composition writing. These include parity of products, interest, timeliness, and prominence given to some forms of argument form [278]. As Carbone suggests, traditionally the rhetorical composition, either in essay or business-letter writing form conformed to the pattern of the five C's – these are – clearness, correctness (force), conciseness, courtesy and character) [279]. The writing skills of the Public Relations practitioner are important but so too are the range of skills which he or she might draw upon in the role -- the critical thinking skills, the planning capabilities, the community and consumer relations, the media persuasion and liaison skills, the reading and spoken comprehension, and good oratory.

Advocacy Writing

Advocacy writing involves objective discussion for a particular cause. In most instances, when writing objectively opinion may only be expressed indirectly however advocacy also involves the positioning of an individual or an organisation amongst its stakeholders or publics, to convey an organizations point of view and to gain confidence or support for a prevailing point of view. Behind any advocacy writing is both situational research and a monitoring of the environment in which an individual or an organisation is situated. The term given for the continual attention as to how an organisation is affected be economic, social, cultural managerial, legal and professional trends and movements is issues management [280]. Issues management involves two methods of calculation, these are firstly, identification; and secondly, anticipation of emerging issues [281]. There are seven methods of research involved in issues management, these are:

- Environmental audits which involve early warning of issues
- Performance perception audits which focus on the individual, group, or organisation itself and the perceptions within it
- Literature reviews which cite references from newspaper magazines, academic journals, government documents and authoritative websites – to look at trends

- Interviews which can be conducted with management, community leaders, media leaders, government officials, customers, stakeholders and employees
- Focus groups which involve small groups of people representing their publics
- Surveys which is a formal research technique to gather information from a variety of correspondents
- Content analysis which involves changing trends in visibility, criticism, perceptions and support [282].

The purpose of these research methods is to analyse issues in trends in the individual, group or organisations environment. Important questions, which need asking, include: What are the causes of the issues? What are the likely impacts? What is the potential for harm? What are the courses of action, which may remediate the issue? Furthermore, what are the issues to those outside the organisation? What are the likely impacts? Concomitant with this aim is to define the various levels of publics in a communication program. Doorley and Garcia have a general formula for Issues Management:

Research / Risk Assessment + Planning Action + Communication + Evaluation = Crisis Avoidance [283]

A likely consequence or cause of action is the production of a position statement. The position statement is what is considered the official position of the organisation and is aligned with the responsibility it has to its wider publics and ultimately to society in general. A position statement has six constituent parts. Firstly, a position paragraph which addresses a complex issue, secondly a position topic which identifies an issue to be addressed, an estimation of the significance and importance of the issue; a statement of the history or background to the information being addressed, a statement of current status to information; and a statement of a projection – how issues are likely to develop [284].

The argumentation structure of a position statement involves a promulgation of the position, an exercise of judgment or opinion, the use of supporting arguments and opposing arguments, a statement of conclusions and recommendations and citations for references consulted [285]. Position statements may be accompanied by organisational statements, which are brief proclamations from an organisation's perspective on timely issues; and by contingency statements, which are written to prepare an organisation for various potential situations that deal with pending scenarios [286].

Chapter 7

'JACK AND THE BEAN STALK': CRISIS MANAGEMENT

'The history of PR is . . . a history of a battle for what is reality and how people will see and understand reality' – Stuart Ewen

The fable of Jack and the bean stork provides a ready analogy for the organisation in crisis – Jack and his widowed mother live in a farm cottage and depend on a dairy cow who stops giving milk. Jack takes the milk to market to be sold but along the way meets a trader who offers to exchange magic beans for the cow. Jack's mother is dismayed when he returns without any money, and Jack throws the beans onto the ground. However, during the night a giant beanstalk grows outside Jack's window. Jack and his mother's original problem has 'grown out of hand' and reaches giant proportions, as has the beanstalk which has grown higher into the sky. Jack climbs the beanstalk high in the sky, and hides in an enormous castle, whose inhabitant is a giant. Returning home the giant smells Jack and threatens to kill him for food. The giantess persuades him not and eventually after the giant falls asleep; Jack steals some coins, and escapes down the beanstalk to his mother. He climbs the beanstalk twice more to steal a goose that lays golden eggs, and a magic harp. The giant awakes and chases Jack down the beanstalk, reaching the ground first, Jack cuts the beanstalk and the giant falls to his death. Jack new about PR! He realised that he had to follow his intuition, and use character, self-knowledge, strength, and to take risks to get he and his mother out of the crisis, brought on by the cow who has stopped giving milk. The problem grew as high as the beanstalk but eventually Jack was equal to it.

Similarly, in a crisis situation, the reputation of an organisation needs protecting, but it also needs to be able to carry out the business and functions for which it is originally intended. It needs to hold true to its purpose. Aside from the crisis event itself and how it is managed by the organisation, crises are damaging to reputation because of the negative information that is generated about an organization during and after them. Both operational and reputational crises can have negative consequences if they are not handled properly. However, careful crisis management can limit the potential damage to a reputation by the projection of a consistent and controlled response to the organisational stakeholders and the wider industry.

Any kind of crisis can threaten to diminish an organisation's reputation. During any crisis, the primary concern is public safety although reputational crises can also be concerned with financial loss, reputational loss, market share, and lawsuits. However, failure to address public safety intensifies the reputational damage of a crisis, which in turn can effect financial reputation. There are three main phases of crises, firstly, the pre-crisis, secondly the crisis response and thirdly post-crisis. Although each phase is critical, the response during the post-crisis phase is critical for preparing for the next crisis. Fourthly of concern is internal crisis communication, which involves how management communicates with an employee about a crisis. Often managers may neglect internal communication in a crisis and need to try harder to communicate corrective actions and accommodate these to their employers. In order to put a positive face on crises, employees need information about actions the organisation takes to address the crises, which may involve both correction and accommodation. Increasingly in today's world of 'instant messaging' and the 'citizen journalist', uses of social media need to be considered and controlled. Crises involve negative consequences such as, firstly, increased damage to an organisation's reputation; secondly, reduced purchase intentions, and thirdly, increased likelihood of customers and publics engaging in negative word of mouth. As Christopher Buckley put it: "[i]n Public Relations, you live with the reality that not every disaster can be made to look like a misunderstood triumph."

The pre-crisis phase involves creating a crisis management plan, selecting and training a crisis management team and conducting exercises to test it. Organisations may want to pre-draft some crises messages. These may be templates used by top management, which are used as news releases and social media channels. The templates include statements by top management, news releases and social media messages (*Tweets, Blogs and Facebook*), and dark web sites, which can be made visble at the appropriate moment. The pre-draft messages save time and add relevant information. The creation of a dark web site that is pre-prepared can anticipate the type of crisis faced, and can be pre-programmed to link with social media channels. The Social Mediated Crisis Communication Model argues that there are three social media channels. Firstly, influential social media creators, or create the crisis information; secondly, social media followers who 'consume' messages from the social media creator; and thirdly, social media inactives who get information from word of mouth social media followers and / or traditional media that report content from influential social media creators. Most crisis communicators have two generic tools available to them – Intranet access which involves suppliers and customers who have direct access to specific stakeholders and may involve enterprise social networking; and a mass notification system with contact information and pre-programmed communication. Using a current website is a good idea, and be prepared to use social media channels in responding to a crisis.

TAKING TO THE MEDIA

- Avoid 'no comment' because it may look like organisation 'guilty' and trying to hide

- Present information clearly and avoid jargon and technical terms
- Maintain strong eye contact, avoid distracting nervous behaviours
- Brief all potential spokespersons on latest crisis information [287].

The three main ‘rules of thumb’ for crisis response are ‘be quick, be accurate, and be consistent’.

When a crisis occurs, an ‘information gap’ is created and people want to know what happened, who it affected, where, and how. If the organisation does not speak to others people with less accurate information will. As Louis Hayes, Jr., noted: *“[a] crisis is a change. More specifically, bad change. In addition, change requires a response. One’s adaptability is a measure of how effective that reaction is.”* Often, the organisation positions itself as a source and presents its side of the story however; pre-drafted messages facilitate a quick response. People want accuracy, they want to know how what happened might affect them and they want a consistent message – IN CLEAR VOICE! Having effective media relations permits crisis managers to reach a wide range of stakeholders fast. In Public Relations, public safety is forefront. People need to know how to protect themselves.

Uses of social media in crises mostly concerns customer service issues. A crisis management team will not be assembled during a *‘Twitter paracrisi’* – which is a term used to describe the way social media influences an emerging crisis. However, social media can have a triggering effect on altering pre-crisis information. Social media has created the need to modify crisis communication in some respects as instant messaging can be multiple and diffuse in effect and constantly updated in ‘real-time’ but previous knowledge can still be viable.

Having a strategy is not a failsafe! You may need to adapt and change. The speed of social media does not replace the need to pursue a specific outcome or the need to develop message to achieve it. In responding to crises, managers need to make deliberate and informed decisions and have responsibilities to a range of stakeholders. Speed is enhanced by crisis information. Social media can provide a data-steam during a crisis, which can be evaluated through examining the quantity and valence (be it emotional tone, or informational credibility) of responses. Crises generate strong emotions – generally either anger, sympathy or anxiety which can be reflected in messaging and then acted upon. Generally, if people support an organisation, they are more likely to have sympathy for it but take negative action if angry or anxious about the organisation. For the Public Relations practitioner, often risk assessment is a routine part of reputation management. A Magnitude Probability Matrix is frequently used (such as the one below which features Jack's Beanstalk'):

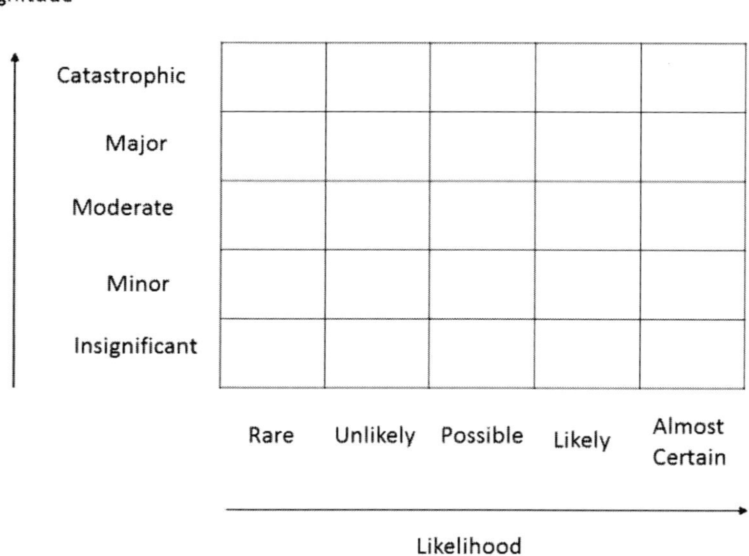

Figure 2. Showing Magnitude / Probability Matrix for Crisis Risk Management [288].

Usually, a repeated crisis is perceived with much more responsibility when an organisation had a previous crisis, or had not known, previously, how to treat its various stakeholders, at different stages of crisis management. So try to learn from mistakes!

Crisis types are given below:

Victim crises – with minimal crisis responsibility

- Natural disasters
- Rumours – false and damaging information
- Workplace violence – attack by former poor current employee on current employees
- Product Tampering/malevolence – in which an external agent causes damage [289].

Accident crises – with low crisis responsibility

- Challenge – stakeholders claim that organisation is operating in an inappropriate manner
- Technical error accidents – equipment technical failure
- Technical error product harm – equipment failure causes a product to be defective

Preventable crises – with strong crisis responsibility.

- Human-error or product harm, (when a product is defective or potentially harmful)
- Organisational misdeed – when management actions put stakeholders at risk [290].

In responding to crises as with consistent performance, Reputation is based on how stakeholders view an organisation. Thus, as a valuable tangible and intangible asset reputation should be protected. The increased organisational responsibility for a crisis results in a greater likelihood of negative word-of-mouth about the organisation and reduced intention to purchase, the goods or services of an organization. Protect the company reputation and you also protect the people and product.

Thus, reputation is maintained or disrupted by the extent towards which blame or responsibility is attributed to the organisation. According to attribution theory, people explain why events occur and attribute responsibility to a situation or person in situation. Attributions inspire emptions and effect how people interact with event and during crises; sometimes during and after crises impacts, blame is attributed to either people or the organisation. Guidelines include:

- All victims or potential victims should receive instructing information, including information recall.
- All victims should be provided an expression of sympathy and information about corrective actions and trauma counselling when needed.
- When there is a crisis of minimal attributions or crisis responsibility and an intensifying factor, then add an excuse and / or justification strategies to instructing information and care responses.
- For crises with low attributions of crisis responsibility and an intensifying factor, adding compensation and or apology strategies to instructing information and care response is recommended [291].

Hence, the third component is an expressive concern or sympathy for the victims who have been hurt or inconvenienced by the crisis. Expressions of concern diminish the reputational damage. Sometimes victim focus is limited to expressions of concern and depending on the magnitude of the event trauma teams will be required to address the needs of employees as well as victims. As Coombs relates, guidelines for reputational management during crises include:

- Making public safety a number one priority
- Using all available communication channels including social media internet
- Providing expression of concern and sympathy for victims
- Providing stress and trauma counselling to victims of crisis and families [292].

Strategies of repairing the reputational damage inflicted on organisations during crises moments (some of which can be drastic and have far reaching impacts) involve determining the basic type of crisis, and considering how the crisis is defined in the media and by stakeholders. Sometimes, quick steps are needed involving limited thin-slice sampling of reactions as well as crisis plans. In responding there are a whole range of options available to the Public Relations practitioner. Which responses are chosen will differ for the severity and magnitude event and the occasion. They may include:

- Confronting or attacking accuser
- Denial – denying there is a crisis
- Scapegoat – blames someone else
- Excuse – minimises organisational responsibility, denying intent to do harm
- Provocation – which is a response to someone else's actions.
- Defensibility – the lack of information about events leading to a crisis.
- Accidental – the lack of control over events leading to crisis, and good intentions.
- Justification – which minimises perceived damage caused
- Ingratiation – which includes praises stakeholders for actions
- Compensation – which includes offers of money and other gifts
- Apology – the organisation takes full responsibility for the crisis and asks for forgiveness [293].

If the crisis is not too severe then add compensation and apology strategies to instructing information, and care responses. In situations where there are strong attributions of crisis responsibility then it is recommended that compensation and apology strategies be combined with instructing information. This may also inspire compassion which is desirable if victims have been created. The compensation strategy is used when victims suffer harm and the reminder and integration strategies can effectively supplement a response, while the denial and 'attack of the accuser' strategies are best used with 'rumour and challenge' crisis responses [294].

During the post-crisis phase, the crisis is no longer centre of attention, and the organisation enters a reputation repair phase in which delivery on informational promises becomes essential or there is a risk of losing the trust of public. The organisation acts to release an update on the recovery process, perform corrective actions or carryout investigations of crisis. Crises should be a learning experience, and people experiencing crises should seek ways to prevent them, including preparation and response. Relatedly, organisations should be encouraged to attend anniversaries and memorials, and deliver all information as promised to stakeholders as soon as is possible, consulting with victims and families to determine an organised role in anniversary events or memorials. It is also an important objective to keep stakeholders up-to-date on the progression of recovery efforts including corrective measures, and to analyse the crisis management effort for lessons and integrate those lessons to organise a crisis management system.

According to Mersham, Theunissen and Peart (2009), in order to produce effective responses during crises Public Relations practitioners need to conduct environmental scans, to be aware of issues of interest, to ensure employees are vigilant and have a plan. In planning for a crisis, it is best to keep a crisis inventory, and a hazard register that records known areas of liability of potential harm [295]. Preparation is paramount. As Mersham et al., (2009) suggest:

- Anticipate issues
- Develop positions
- Identify publics and policies
- Identify desired behaviours
- Monitor business environment
- Prioritise issues
- Analyse

- Decide on strategy
- Implement plan
- Evaluate plan [296].

The organisation might ask itself: What has happened, what is the organisation doing about it? How does the organisations feel about it; is it effecting others? Are others talking with us now whose perceptions we can influence? Will we seem less compassionate and caring if we respond later as opposed to quickly? If we delay any longer how difficult would it be to influence the outcome?

The crisis response communication plan aims to target publics and change perceptions. The crisis team are usually comprised of a senior manager, a communications expert, a human resources safety person, a lawyer, an operations person, an engineer and a technical person. They are drawn together to established purpose of plan, including the company philosophy, an explanation of specific responsibilities, the exchange of communication contacts, a listing of emergency personnel, and physical description of on-site off-site crisis control. The media response plan includes a delineation of responsibilities, and pre-prepared press releases. Other communication activities of the crisis network include preparing a training plan, plan manual, emergency response, testing programme, testing of alert system, essential information, guidelines in crisis, and communications activities for follow up.

During a crisis as Mersham, et al. state:

- Follow an action plan
- Gather and understand
- Agree on strategy
- Put the public first
- Prepare a media statement
- Brief a chosen spokesperson
- Decide what resources you will need
- Use website to post information.

- Brief employees
- Be flexible
- Communicate
- Be truthful with yourself
- Maintain eye contact with an interviewer
- Pick winners; decide whose side you are on? [297].

Hence if there is a crisis situation, it is better to be open and honest, if apologies are necessary make them, and if you have plan that you can bring into action all the better. Treat people well and you will manage your way through to the best outcome. As Doorley and Garcia note, the 'rule of 45 Minutes, 6 Hours, 3 days, and Two Weeks' may apply – whereby the ability to influence stakeholder reactions diminishes with temporal distance from the crisis event. Reacting within 45 Minutes to define the crisis and react, often leads to early dissipation of negativity. If this is not accomplishable, it may produce averagely six hours of discomfort and distress as people share information, which has not been replied to; after three days media saturation will begin to take hold, and depending on the magnitude of the crisis, it may linger for several days. The longer a crisis is left without reaction, the more people will become involved and the more difficult it will be to resolve [298, 313, 314].

Chapter 8

'SHADES OF GREY (AND GREEN)': CORPORATE CITIZENSHIP

'Without publicity there can be no public support, and without public support every nation must decay' – Benjamin Disraeli

Public Relations is people and organisation focused. Organisations cannot function without some sort of organised relationship internal or external. Just and respectful behaviours in turn enliven the inter-activity of the organisation and help to maintain the health of its corporate culture [298]. The aim of any modern professional workplace is the fulfilment of individual and organisational goals within an equitable environment characterised by fairness. Hence corporate responsibility is increasingly seen as a 'throughout organisation' process, effecting stakeholders, clients and employees. In today's business world, organisations and corporates are increasingly seeing and, more importantly, reporting on, a wide range of measures that generate a complete picture of their activities. Clients, stakeholders, chief operating officers, and shareholders and employees, are increasing asking more of their organisations, they want corporate responsibility – so called – triple bottom line measures. Reporting on corporate responsibility involves the Public Relations practitioner in a range of activities that crystallise in a set of attitudinal behaviours:

- Get facts
- Engage critics
- Demonstrate
- Earn credibility
- Connect to business strategy
- Be transparent [299].

Where once business organisations were motivated only by profit, increasingly they are reporting their social and environmental responsibilities also. Ideally, organisations may strive for a cognitively perfect situation in which employees are offered optimum quality of life, and can be enriched by the experience of workplace fairness, as well as delivering company objectives [300]. Nevertheless, this is an aspiration for most organisations, and few organisations would actually achieve it. A healthy internal culture and an awareness of principles of organisational justice can minimise aberrant behaviours, which may cause harm to reputation and make public relations issues easier to manage. Perceptions of fairness can help employees to identify with their jobs and contribute based on citizen-like behaviours, which may lend themselves to organisational consolidation [301].

Organisational citizenship behaviours are a subset of human resources in which equal treatment, salary-levels; decision-making, interpersonal behaviours, work relationships, and tolerance for moral and social perspectives are part of the social fabric [302]. These themselves are a subset of that utopian feature of cosmopolitanism which sees the ". . . end-point of human societal evolution [as] a condition where different human communities . . . live together without conflict arising between them" [303]. The cosmopolitanism of 'civilisation' identity is increasingly important in the globalised world. As Samuel Huntington (1993) observes it will be shaped by, ". . . the interactions among seven or eight major civilizations. These include Western, Confucian, Japanese, Islamic, Hindu, Slavic-Orthodox, Latin American, and possible African civilization" [304]. These citizens of this new cosmopolitan order will be a part of a 'pan-ethnic- religious-national' world. They will be as much a part of transnational organisations as they will be citizens of globalised nation states. While being culturally different from one-another, they will nevertheless share some cognitive and cultural traits, because of the homogenisation of international spaces.

Organisational 'health' is the product of a wide variety of factors that involve embracing some important maxims of reputational management – those of being open and honest, and striving for continuous improvement. These corporate may also be larger social, societal or civic goals. Organisations may strive to achieve their goals, mission and objectives and in so doing participate in a wider movement of corporate responsibility and corporate citizenship. Leadership and customer satisfaction are important heuristics in organisational decision making as they drive the perception of justice in organisational citizenship behaviours. To attain excellence in leadership and customer satisfaction, a safe environment is a necessary, but not sufficient criterion. Social exchange theory[2] posits that human behaviour is premised on an economic interest to maximise rewards, minimise losses and support workplace interactions [305]. Whilst organisational justice is about perceptions of fairness and equality at work, it is also concerned with "the rules developed to distribute or to take decisions on distributions of acquisitions such as goods, services, rewards, punishments, wages, organisational positions, opportunities and roles among employees and societal norms that constitute the basis for these rules" [306]. The negotiation of these rules is an integral part of organisational fairness and directly informs perceptions of organisational culture.

According to Hoy and Tarter (2004), there are eight principles of organisational justice [307]. The principles are:

- Equality – contributions in proportion to incomes
- Perception – effect of general perception on justice

[2] Social exchange theory is used in psychology and sociology as a concept which explains social stability and change as a process of negotiation. It is a quasi-economic theory in so much as it presupposes that human relationships use a 'subjective cost-benefit' analysis to make rational choices between a comparison of alternatives. Early proponents of social exchange theory were Thibaut and Kelley in their 1959 text, *The social psychology of groups*.

- Polyphony – increase in decision making increase in fair decisions
- Interpersonal justice – respectful, kind, mature behaviours
- Consistency – consistency in leader's behaviours
- Political and social equality – share collective organisational mission
- Correction – amelioration of wrong or bad decisions

If as Rapport states, "[t]he concept (cosmopolitan) expressed a tension: to be human was at once to inhabit an individual embodiment, a particular spatiality and temporality (or 'polis'), and to be an essential instantiation of species-wide capabilities and liabilities, part of the human whole (or 'cosmos') then this entails an ontology 'state of being' and a relationship with others governed by rule-making behaviours" [308]. When citizenship and cosmopolitanism are seen as contributing at the organisational level, there are also at least four types of justice involved in organisational citizenship behaviour (OCB): Firstly, distributive justice, which involves fairness about organisational outcomes; secondly, procedural justice which is concerned with the concept of an individual's assessment about right and wrong of procedural methods; thirdly, interactional justice which involves the interpersonal treatment received during procedures (the relationship between employee and employer); fourthly, organisational citizen discretionary behaviour (outside the formal reward system), which promotes the functioning of the organisation [309]. Such behaviours may include altruism[3] and helping, courtesy, conscientiousness, civic virtue and sportsmanship, which may imply refraining from complaint about trivialities [310]. Fairness assumes a level of consistency, bias suppression, accuracy and correctability. The loss of trust in perceptions of unfairness results in reversion to contract before counter-productive behaviours [311]. The perception of justice involves psychic energy, altruism, an expanding consciousness, a drive for interest and self-esteem] [312].

---

[3] Altrusim is defined as an attitude of caring about others, the opposite of self-centredness. The word was invented by Auguste Combte as an antonym of egoism, from the Latin *alteri* meaning 'others' or 'somebody else'.

As Sison (2011) points out, corporations, as legal entities carrying out particular goals, only exist because of people, nevertheless they are collective instruments comprised of individual citizens tasked to achieve goals unachievable otherwise. Citizenship lends corporations a sense of identity, community membership and a justification for rights and responsibilities as "secondary citizens" [313]. While a citizen participates in deciding what is good in society, aristocracies are based on excellence and trust (and oligarchies are based on wealth). The liberal model of citizenship stresses negative freedoms of oppression and arbitrary rules; while the civic-minded focus on active participation in a common good by fostering community ties [314]. Corporations participate in governing or the sharing of governance in developed political systems, and assume neo-governmental roles within aspects of some economic activities [315]. Corporations arguably administer citizenship as employee rights. These may include considerations such as Remuneration, working conditions, and health and education. However, when government regulation is weak and/or the welfare state is in retreat, corporations may instead assume some of the burdens of ensuring basic rights [316]. Notions of citizenship involve psychological security. Psychological security includes such behaviours as non-interference, self-mastery, non-domination, empathetic social relations, and a comprehensive corporate polity and governance. Liberal minimalism emphasises contractual rights and duties, fair wages, healthy and safe working conditions and freedom from discrimination for acceptable work quality [317]. Organisational citizenship behaviour involves community helping, sportsmanship-like initiative, the practice of an 'intrinsic quality' such as virtue and an objective dimension such as external goods and service improvements in knowledge skills and habits [318].

The growth of corporate citizenship is also sometimes coterminous with uncertainties about the location of civic 'goods,' especially those concerning the social responsibilities of business and the power of corporations, which redefine the norms of citizenship and of human rights. There are different views of citizenship:

- Liberal minimalist
- Civic republicanism
- Developmental
- Deliberative

Under the tenets of liberal minimalism, citizens need protection from arbitrary rule and oppression by government [319]. Citizenship may be ethically based on either rights or utilitarian approaches. For John Locke (1690), citizenship described the rights that people were entitled to, including those fundamental civil responsibilities of 'life, liberty, and property' and it was the duty of government to secure it, when the individual was not able to [320]. If the government did not secure those benefits, the people could withhold their consent for government. While both free expression of preferences in markets (invisible hand) and public good contribute to the objectives of governance as forms of citizen behaviours. The tenets of civic republicanism provide for equal rights and political equality (as with liberal minimalism) but also prize civic good which is underpinned by a set of communitarian ties or 'moral bonds' that provide a motivational basis for civic virtue. These include obligations such as obeying the law, paying taxes, and performing jury duty or military service. This civic framework needs to inform the awareness of the public relations practitioner and reputation manager.

For many organisations, even stridently independent trans-national corporations, government is also a stakeholder (if only by virtue of the tax take). Developmental democracy, on the other hand, requires that citizens who are highly participatory and have very close bonds with one another to engage in partnerships, which are the principal means of personal and intellectual development. A triple bottom line (social justice, environmental responsibility, economic development) is predicated on the assumption that business provides a major contribution to society through long-term commitment [321]. The critical assessment of relations between corporations and governments and the notion of developmental democracy (a matter of delegating responsibility for governance) is a contested issue; citizens' rights are delivered as the result of the expectation that people become active protagonists in the governance process [322]. In a deliberative democracy, there is an emphasis on citizen participation in public affairs and an assumption that people participate in a deliberative fashion. Such deliberative approaches may address issues of complexity, pluralism, inequality and decision-making [323]. However, as Brian Eno cautions: "[w]hen governments rely increasingly on sophisticated Public Relations agencies; public debate disappears and is replaced by competing propaganda campaigns, with all the accompanying deceits. Advertising isn't about truth or fairness or rationality, but about mobilising deeper and more primitive layers of the human mind."

Table 3. Showing types of citizenship [325]

Types of Citizenship	Nature of citizenship	Nature of participation by citizenship
Liberal Minimalism	Rights or utilities, administered by governing elites	Extremely limited; mostly by electoral choice of governing elites
Civic Republicanism	Participation in a community, obligations towards the public (or 'civic') good	Obligation to governments Sharing governance with elites Pressure group activity Direct participation in governing
Developmental Democracy	Network of interpersonal relations in society for individual and social flourishing.	Obligations to society Relations to fellow citizens
Deliberative Democracy	Free deliberation over public decisions in a community	Collective problem-solving on basis of equality Plural values to address complex problems

Participatory models of citizenship which don't necessarily reflect participation in their own operations but which represent interests that transcend aggregates of individual citizens valorise societal organisations' engagement in governance. However, corporations also represent aggregates of human interests (which include shareholders, consumers, employees, business customers), and as such, governance is a form of surrogate citizenship [324].

Employees engage in both Organisational Citizen Behaviours (OCB) and Counterproductive Work Behaviours (CWB), which can be risky for reputation management. Sometimes excessive morally praiseworthy behaviours, or over-praising good behaviours, can lead to a moral licence to behave immorally [326]. Organisational Citizen Behaviours maintain and enhance the social and psychological context and support task performance [327]. Both OCB and Counterproductive Work Behaviours can result in the pursuit of positive affect and future satisfaction [328]. In weak cosmopolitanism there is an equal concern shown for all persons in the world, however strong cosmopolitanism adds the requirement that everyone is subjected to equal treatment [329]. Furthermore, the 'unfair disadvantage argument' holds that it is unfair to treat people differently for things that they are not responsible for. Hence there is a form of 'global luck egalitarianism' that is similar to the Rawlsian 'veil of ignorance'[4] [330]. On the other hand there is no injustice in inequality between nations or states, provided certain minimal conditions are met (for example, everyone has the means for self-determination or decent minimum conditions are upheld) [331]. Consequently, a major tenet of cosmopolitanism is that of 'equal consideration.' This is a principle that the reputation manager and public relations practitioner should bear in mind when conceptualising corporate engagement. In other words, nationality is considered a happenstance and people may be differentiated by responsibility considerations in which need is the morally relevant 'driver.' Morally upright people sometimes chose to engage in a limited amount of what could be immoral behaviours [332]. Both organizational citizen

[4] The 'veil of ignorance' is a thought experiment which is used for determining the morality of an issue. People in the 'original position' know nothing about their position in the social order. When selecting principles for the distribution of rights and resources in a society, this 'veil of ignorance' prevents them from knowing what their own position will be. Thus people who are subject to the 'veil of ignorance' will make choices that are based on moral principles rather than self-interest. Rawls, John (1999). *A Theory of Justice*. Harvard University Press.

behaviours (OCB) and Counterproductive Work behaviours (CWB) can result in the pursuit of positive affect and future satisfaction, which deviates from a moral ideal because the view of self is not tied to a particular decision but to a moral balance [333].

Cosmopolitanism is defining the terms of a global era in which national borders and differences are dissolving [334]. Advanced modern nations may have a globalising dimension which instantiates the capacity of governments and trans-national corporations to stretch across the globe [335]. A cosmopolitan is seen as an acrobat, a term that reflects boundary manipulation, implies mobility of culture and pan-ethnic dynamics, infers global inequality, reconfigures class politics in territorialised society and speaks of a world citizenship [336]. External or cosmopolitan forces and internal national forces can be in collusion or in collision, which involves describing differing dynamics in local and global national and transitional situations, which may or may not be interlocking in forms of civic stratification [337]. For Lockwood inequalities are embedded in the practice of citizenship, a citizenship that is as likely as class relations to structure group interests [338] are. A post-national[5] society, which occurs in those nations whose trade regulations are the most relaxed, blurs the boundaries between a citizen and non-citizen, granting or denying the right tool of governance [339]. As Morris states, there is a distinction between public opinion and public interest; the rights which structure relations among individuals and social organisations and the protection of rights in the public interest [340]. A public sphere has the potential to mediate between global and national citizenship and loosen the regimented ties between democratic legitimacy and state organisation [341]. Calloni argues that the term 'cosmopolite' is composed of two Greek words *cosmos* and *politike*, meaning 'human being.' A citizen of cosmos combines the existence of a citizen (belonging to polis) with idea of cosmos creating a harmonic system [342]. A citizen is someone who does not have to

[5] Postnationalism is the process by which nation statesand identities can lose their consideration relative to globalization. Globalizing economic factors have shifted attention away from cultural differences of nationalisties and obnto shred efficiencies of trade. Political power has shifted from nation formation to supernational entities such as the European Union and the United Nations.

reference his/her political belonging in terms of specific political borders but assumes an individualised being living in communities, denoted by borders and respected based on rights and duties [343]. Kantian normative cosmopolitanism is based on world citizenship and universal hospitality to foreigners and politics grounded on a dialectic between inclusion /exclusion. A global civil society has a top-down and universal values system and a bottom-up human rights, democracy, dignity, freedom, and equality approach [344]. However, increasingly these desirable goals of a democratic civil society may only be achieved with 'buy in' from companies, business and organisations, who reflect wider aims of corporate responsibility – environmental and social. Added to concerns with marking profits which motivate business (or in reaching organisational targets, for non-profit making organisations) are targets, and aims in social and environmental gaols – 'triple-bottom-line' reporting. Slowly enforcement and regulation is being replaced by emphasis on education and training, as guiding motivation of the responsible company.

To this end, developments such as the 'Guiding Principles on Business and Human Right's' developed in 2011 by the United Nations Human Rights Council, promote two factors in organisational performance. These are 'due diligence' in which organisations strive to prevent and mitigate any human rights risks and to look for impacts on human rights of organisational activities; and secondly, transparency, in which organisations track human rights performances [345]. Triple bottom line reporting aims above to provide accurate information, on targets and measures, which are assessable and relevant to give a full picture of organisations actions. As Doorley and Garcia (2011) relate, corporate responsibility involves six main factors:

- Prioritising issues
- Contextualising objectives and strategy
- Referencing good practice
- Providing accurate detail
- Measuring current activities and projecting future impacts
- Acknowledging obstacles [346].

A pro-active reputation manager will constantly put these six principles in action.

Green Market Business

Increasingly and as a consequence of triple-bottom-line organisational responsibility, entities are coming under pressure to reflect values of sustainability and to be environmentally friendly, over and above their profit-making purpose – they are asked to advocate a 'green (or carbon neutral) footprint. Green-consumerism holds that market processes and the consumption-decisions of millions of individuals can on their own create an environmentally sustainable society. A central idea of the market economy is that one kind of resource starts becoming scarce, price will go up. Yet many sustainable resources, some of which we might take for granted, such as water, air, food are needed by all. As we already know quality of life is uneven in many parts of the world, the industrial north can play a leadership role in sustainable business practices and at the same time teach and provide innovative technologies for sustainable systems in the developing world.

A counterpoint to this is the unproven belief that the market may be a self-balancing system. If the market is analogous to ecological systems themselves, will solutions found by relying on local-knowledge and the intelligence of individuals and less on state intervention? Yet how viable is the concept of effortless 'ecological modernisation'? Under a regime of modernisation, environmental standards may gradually be raised, resulting in ecological modernisation [347].

Correspondingly, Beck also suggests that we live in an age of manufactured risk - risk is no longer an act of god, but of science-based intervention in the natural world (solving social and economic problems). As such, science and politics in our 'second modernity' [348] Beck further suggests that new forms of reflexivity are developing in which people are losing faith in all forms of authority (including scientific enterprise) and create their own understandings. Increasingly, at least in the developed world the ‘new individualism’ is part of a global citizenship. This includes the proliferation of green technologies on a local scale. However, this is counter-balanced by the need to maintain communities of sustainable integration. Brown, who claims, that socialism collapsed because it did not allow the market to tell economic truth, gives a warning that capitalism may collapse because it does not allow the market to tell the ecological truth [349]. Hence, the reputation of organisations is increasingly concerned with maintaining a respect for the environment in which they operate, a principle that also concerns the public relations strategist. Organisations need to inform their publics what they are doing right, as much as they need to safeguard and plan for what can go wrong.

Chapter 9

'IMAGE OR REALITY?': BRANDING AND REPUTATION

'The keys to brand success are self-definition, transparency, authenticity and accountability' – Simon Mainwaring

The three primary axes of reputation management – organisational image, organisational identity and organisation reputation – are influenced by factors both internal and external to the business or organisation [350]. Hence, reputation management is primarily concerned with the development of an organisation's intangible capital – the way in which its positive attributes can be leveraged to increase its market share and appeal. As Brian Greene notes: *"[b]uilding a brand through effective storytelling is at the heart of what PR professionals do."* But brand is also related to reputation – much as the semiologist's 'signifier' to the signified'. When you recognise a symbol, you want to know what it means; it is Public Relations and marketing strategists' aim to make that connection between brand and company image and reputation both positive and instant for the public and the consumer. However, reputation itself is a more complex term and can signify the outcome – perceptions and impressions – of a whole range of interactions through time.

A definition provided by Fombrun (1996) states that corporate reputation is "a perceptual representation of a company's past actions and future prospects that describe the firm's overall appeal to all its key constituents when compared to other leading rivals" [351]. Reputation management is characterised by organisational attributes and the myriad relationships that organisations form with and between staff, clients, stakeholders, and their perceived value as both affective and effective competencies. It is both a form of evaluation and of agency – a measure of an organisation's performance over time (what it is and does and how it behaves) but to staff, consumers and stakeholders it may be a perceptual representation of both past actions and future events – what it is possible for someone to do with an organisation. Dowling (2001) proposes three questions that form the IDU test for an organisation's reputation management [352]. These three questions are:

- Is what your organisation does important to their customers?
- Can your organisation really deliver a valuable product and / or service?
- Is what your organisation provides unique?

An organisation, which cannot answer these questions, will not be as well purposed or branded as one that can. Reputation is a marketplace affordance which is in part based on a gauge of the organisation's standing (as a component of the ability of those internal to the organisation to bring positive benefit to those external to it) and hence may represent (aside from critical imaging of marketing) the cumulative regard (either positive or negative) of an organisation's constituent group over time. The result is a synthesis of opinions, perceptions and attributes, an evaluation (which may be fleeting or lengthy) of the 'bank' of information about a firm, a socially constructed 'collective memory' as a form of intangible output which describes its future and past characteristics. At the level of social interaction reputational concern might be expressed through behaviours of ingratiation, some forms of downward presentation (e.g., apology, modesty, depreciation), which conversely often produce positive attitudes in the receiver and enhance reputation. Flattery too is a form of ingratiation and reputation management [353]. At the basis of interaction between people is the thought and behaviour that many people find social interchange rewarding and therefore this is a stimulus for reputation (management). Reputation management thus acts as a triggering and moderating topic for inter-organisational relationships and exchange [354].

Consequently, one of the first tasks any analysts of reputation management might perform is to identify the characteristics of an organisation that contribute to its profile and reputation. Osgood, Suci and Tannenbaum (1975) identify three dimensions along which the reputation of an organisation may be valued [355]. These are first an evaluative dimension – which stimulates either positive or negative reactions; second a potency dimension – how strong or weak are the perceptions, emotions and beliefs created by the organisation; and third, an activity dimension – is the company's image a causal factor in the behaviour of others? A fourth dimension, the utilitarian function can also be added – how useful is the organisation to people in achieving their goals and ambitions? However, fifth, sixth and seventh dimensions might also supplement this model: an associative dimension – to what extent is the organisation associated with other organisations, how well are its products and services, understood, is it a market leader, a market definer, or a market 'computer'; sixth, a credibility and congruency dimension – are the organisation's marketing claims for itself credible, how well are they believed, how likely is interacting with the organisation to achieve what the organisation's claims for its clients and service-users; and seventh, a value-expressive function how likely is the organisation to meet the clients' values and motivations. Thus, reputation management can be thought of as a multi-layered social, media, business, and intangible construction that is derived from the myriad associations and potential interactions that staff, clients, stakeholders and potential audiences have with it.

Reputation management interactions or the myriad interpersonal interactions that clients, staff and stakeholders have with organisations take on a variety of characteristics, forms, experiences, expressions and emotions. These take place on a spectrum between utility and sentimentality – from the customer who may only buy products and watch brand marketing, to employees who receive payment in exchange for services and some forms of property and who fulfil many functions – some utilitarian (based on transacted value given and received), some deontological (based on activity with a moral purpose), to work experiences that give clients and employees meaning, expression and emotion (intangible capital benefits). However, it is in the differences in associated meanings produced on this spectrum by companies that the intangible capital of reputation management may be perceived, experienced, leveraged and marketed. As Kong and Farrell (2010) suggest, "Organisations are more likely to grow and develop higher performance potential if more resources are added in image and reputation" [356].

Reputation management analysts are compelled to search for the 'essence', which makes an organisation successful; this is often hard to discover. Some organisations have great products but a low-profile leadership, some have good services but little identifiable market profile, others have an ability to blend in to the cultural consciousness of the time and deliver products and services which have a seamless integration in the social fabric of business communities – such organisations may also have relatively longer corporate lives. So too do organisations which manage risk better through time. As Doorley and Garcia (2015) state: "effective corporate responsibility improves the bottom line by managing risk. Market-based pressure poses the risk of lower sales and a higher cost of capital. Legal pressure presents the risk of liability and less operating flexibility. Public pressure puts at risk a company's most valuable intangible assets – corporate reputation and brand equity. All of these risks, if left unmanaged, can affect company financials." [357]. However, often too the common dominator of successful companies is to produce a 'social effect' – either to deliver an identity –relation within the organisation among employees or to deliver it outside the organisation in terms of goods and services. However, corporate reputation often involves another factor – the degree of esteem that the organisation is held in (that may be attributable to a variety of factors) which is the result of a complex confluence of internal organisational and external communication factors; these coalesce into what is known as 'brand reputation' – the degree of 'identifiability' and commodity desirability an organisation may be known by. Trust and dependability are also important factors in brand reputation but corporate reputation is not just a series of linear relationships between product and services, managers, employees and clients but also predicated on corporate values and the integrity of business relationships. Thus, it could be argued that the organisation produces an overall 'consciousness' in which reputation is in a constant state of creation, flux, and wane, related to both social responsibility and the desire for meaning [358]. However, reputation management can be fickle, as the adage goes: "It takes a lifetime to build a reputation and only a few seconds to destroy one." A 'values-centred' organisation, for example, will be identifiable as a seller 'of goodness' across the range of employees and to the client market. While reputation management is, essential to any functional organisation there is a lingering uncertainty among some businesses (usually successful businesses) that to need to actively market a business is tantamount to admitting deficiency in some regard. After all, if the client base is regular, why the need to? Similarly, many businesses spend thousands of dollars on marketing to recruit new clients while some might be better spent on retaining existing customers.

Corporate Reputation

As Sherofsky (1997) points out, one of the fundamental contributing factors to corporate performance and reputation is human nature itself and the reputation of organisations is comprised of hierarchies of address between clients /customers, staff / workers, and managers, which produce socially constructed negotiated meanings which may impact on local, national or international myths [359]. This negotiated meaning has been characterised as a 'capture desire or struggle' that takes place around 'public and private energy fields' as the different agents and actors associated with an organisation interact in its business [360]. However, it would be too simplistic to regard reputation management is a matter of 'setting organisational course' and continuing 'plain sailing' as often meanings in organisations may arise out of 'agonistic tension' [361]. Brand awareness and brand reputation arise out of the construction of meaning which emerges through social construction. As Burnier (2005) states, "[f]or interactionists, the on-going social (or political) dynamics of persistence and change and of stability and emergence suggest a social (or political) order that is 'negotiated'" [362]. Another way of conceptualising brand reputation is provided by Zabala et al. (2005), who regard the 'intangible asset' of brand reputation as the relational difference between the market price of a company and its book value [363]. Corporate reputation is thus in part determined by stakeholder recognition of a company, through the representation of its staff and functions, products and services and the credibility and management of the intangible assets of the company – goodwill, staff morale, consumer satisfaction, for example. Zabala et al. (2005), emphasise the importance of the congruency or continuity between internal and external company behaviours and shared values between staff and consumers [364].

If an organisation has, basic high levels of trust – internally with staff and externally with stakeholders, it less easy for reputational crises to cause lasting damage, giving rise to the adage: "By the time you hear the thunder, it's too late to build the ark." However, when they do occur, Gonxalez-Herroro and Pratt (1996) suggest that there is a four-step model to implement, which consists of: issues management, planning prevention, crisis strategy, and post-crisis activities [365]. It is a characteristic of media 'storms' involving company reputations to change over either short or longer durations, hence a key feature of any strategy is to develop a system of intervention to bring about proactive (positive) change [366]. Honesty followed by remediation is a straightforward step in encouraging positive reputation management. Maintaining positive media relations and providing contexts for identified issues are two further steps that may be taken to ameliorate reputation crises. According to Coombs (1999), there are seven possible communication steps to maintain brand reputation: attack the accuser, denial, excuse, justification, ingratiation, corrective action, and full apology [367]. Which of these methods are deployed is situation-dependent. In conclusion, Scott and Walsham (2005) argue that reputation "has been a key resource, shaping commercial choices throughout history") [368]. They also identify three main components to reputation management: creditworthiness (honouring contracts), aesthetic components (identity, image, and brand); social responsibility and business ethics [369]. Hence, corporate reputation is regarded as being a 'strategic construct' [370]. On the one hand, brand reputation can be a valuable asset and contribute to the longevity of a company; on the other hand, it can also be fragile and easily damaged. However, arguably the single most tangible feature within the 'intangible asset' of corporate reputation and brand management is the shared agency between the agents and actors who interact within the ambit of the organisation in the market place.

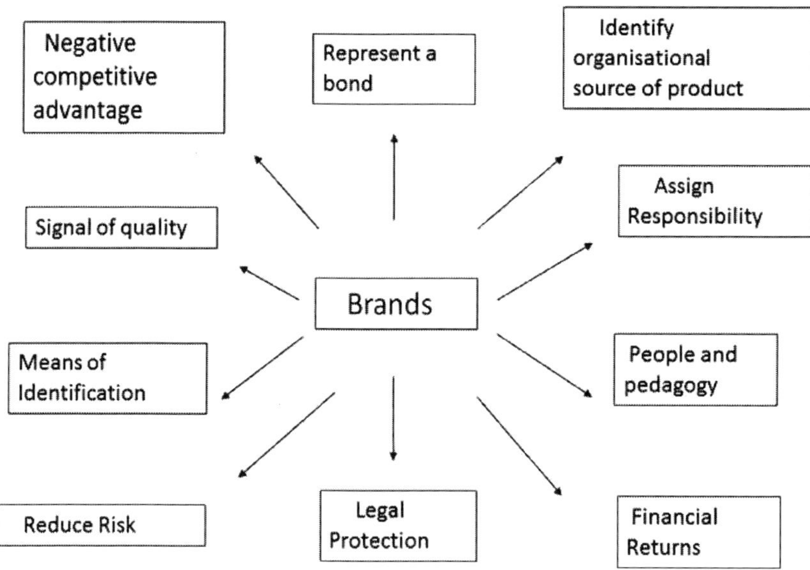

Figure 2. Depicting the various impact factors that brand management has on marketplace behaviours.

Whilst the organisational brand is the signifier of the organisation's identity and market place relevance, its overall reputation is assessment of organisation's quality derived from many stakeholders. For Doorley and Garcia *reputation* is the sum of an organisation's performance, behaviour and communications alongside an assessment of how 'authentic' the organisation is to its mission. This is popularly given the formulaic expression of:

Reputation = (Performance + Behaviour + communications X authenticity factor [371]

Increasingly for many organisations in the developed West and also in the Western influenced developing world, performance is not only about profit (or achieving target measures if a not-for-profit organisation) but also about corporate responsibility involving 'triple bottom line' measuring, or registering and improving how the corporation or organisation responds to wider social or cultural or civic responsibilities. An organisation that achieves a large profit may be celebrated in business but could be socially and culturally unacceptable if it behaves poorly in doing so. An organisation that consumes too much of a common good will for example, receive much critique, despite its popularity with shareholder. To achieve solid and consistent reputations, organisations need to tell stakeholders and publics what they are doing, and it needs to tell them this clearly and effectively. An organisations activities which are not known, will be hard to recognise and hard to define, and could even attract the wrong kind of attention for this reason – despite the glib belief that the best companies are those which no one ever sees! Organisations also need to devote time and attention with their stakeholders – this will include internal staff, customers, consultants and other clients. If stakeholder relationships are positive and open, and communications clear, then a good reputation will follow if an organisation is consistent in its actions and behaviours. Finally, an organisation needs to be authentic, its performance, behaviours, communications, and actions need to be clearly aligned, they need to 'make sense' and to be consistent, if they are customers, clients and other stakeholders will appreciate the coherence of the company brand. Organisations may be assessed by benchmarking against a combination of objective and subjective measures. As mentioned previously, these are reflected in the Harris-Fombrun quotient, which has six measures of reputation: emotional appeal, products and services, vision and leadership, workplace environment, financial performance, social responsibility [372].

If we join the terms 'organisational consciousness' and 'social responsibility' together we might get the term 'corporate responsibility.

That corporates have social and environmental responsibilities beyond those of making profits for shareholder and stakeholders is implicit with any practice of triple bottom line management. 'Corporate responsibility' is also a theory of reputational management but it is debatable whether it is yet a core theory. Having said that, leadership tends to place a high priority, increasingly, on corporate responsibility and its importance is growing as an indicator of business vitality. Ever since Robert Owen's model factories of new Lanark near the falls of the Clyde River in Scotland in the early nineteenth century (See Owen's Statement Regarding New Lanark, published in 1812) it has been shown that acting responsibly as an employer actually dies optimise corporate functioning in some ways. However, another view holds that most corporations are 'neutral' in their values, and they exist only for business purposes, and mainly for profit making.

Corporate responsibility is relevant to reputation management in that it involves communications and being sensitive to market indicators and criticism and feedback. Arguably, corporate responsibility is also important economically, particularly in the long term, with its emphasis on respecting relationships between stakeholders. The global financial crisis of 2008, for example, could be said to have occurred (in the broad sense) because lending was well regulated, that is, corporate responsibility was not practiced within a suitable framework. However, it is also debatable whether corporate responsibility means something more than reporting to regulatory requirements and ensuring that the industry maintains such an environment for good business. Any investment in reputation management requires ethics, and ethics is inherent to communicating and in turn requires truthfulness and transparency. Communication about reputation requires credibility and a 'climate of belief'. Credibility also involves truthfulness and falsity. Beal, Goyen and Philips (2005) argue that financial returns, non-wealth-related returns, or social change are not sufficient motives behind ethical investing, for example – there is a third dimension termed 'ethicalness' [373] Individuals choose to invest based on their 'indifference plane' which reflects utility as an expected return on risk within an assessment of ethicalness. As Russell and Brockman (2011) state: "[i]nvestments made in firms labelled as sound corporate citizens benefit from investors from both a return and risk perspective while providing cognitive externalities as well" [374]. Hence the good corporate citizen is seen as a better bet, because their reputation is for sound business practice that is also socially and environmentally more responsible.

Chapter 10

'SQUARE PEGS AND ROUND HOLES': INTANGIBLE VALUE

'If I was down to my last dollar, I would spend it on Public Relations' – Bill Gates

To a phlegmatic reductionist, reputational value is a tangible asset something appreciated as if it can be touched, tasted, seen and heard, and is seen as inseparable from the physical operation of the organization itself; in others, the reputation derived from careful Public Relations and reputational management is an 'intangible asset' something ephemeral but highly appreciated like esteem itself, that permeates how people experience the organization, and is the 'stock' of regard or appreciation, people have about an organization. It's more fun to view many aspects of Public Relations and reputation management as an 'intangible asset' that is, like intellectual property itself, or goodwill in customer relations, something that can be changed and reshaped along with an organization but which nevertheless permeates its physical or virtual presence. The *Nike swoosh* is synonymous for example, with the company mantra of '*Just do it'*. If human-like creatures beamed down to earth and examined our billboards and even graffiti for signs of our culture, they might think that the *Nike* mantra and sign were the symbols of a global religion, or even that the human diet was based on apples grown by an elderly man with a beard, glasses and quizzical expression. Such is power that some brands have to saturate our communities and cities that they become super-saturated, ubiquitous and the symbolism tends to lose its meaning until it is re-imagined anew. Yet, Intangibles are defined as '. . . assets that one cannot see or touch, such as patents and goodwill, but that become relevant when they are the subjects of a market transaction.' [375]. Zambon offers a further definition: "[i]ntangible assets can be defined as a source of future benefits that is without a physical embodiment." For example, intellectual property is an intangible asset with legal rights. This definition includes innovation-related intangibles (research and development patents), but also market-related (brands), human resource (competencies, skills and training), and organizational intangibles (internal structures, systems, procedures, routines, and processes). A significant distinction can be drawn between 'hard' intangibles, which are tradable in the market place, and 'soft' intangibles, which cannot be sold or negotiated [376]. As John Kay explains:

> The modern economy has many different kinds of distinctive capabilities and so many different kinds of intangible assets: competitive advantages based on brands or reputations with groups of customers; strategic assets such as patents and copyrights or local monopolies; structures of relationships with suppliers or employees. 'Our people are our greatest asset' is a cliché of company reports, and there is a lot in it. All of these factors explain why the value of companies is greater than the value of their tangible assets [377].

An organization's reputation has an intangible value. It is earned by performance over time, and cannot be properly measured largely because those who attempt to measure it are themselves being measured to form it. Reputation is fluid and is not static, it is dynamic and a change in the organization's performance can lead it to go up of down. It therefore requires managing as a strategic asset, "an intangible yet powerful tool that can contribute significantly to the company's bottom line" [378]. Intangibles can also be deployed in multiple issues. An example, which

Daniel Andriessen uses, is that, '[a]lthough an airplane can be used during a time period on one route only, its reservation system can serve, at the same time, a potentially unlimited number of customers.' [379]. As well as profiting from 'network effects', they are frequently characterized by large fixed costs and minimal marginal costs and thus increasing rather than decreasing returns [380].

Lower prices encourage consumption and discourage increasing production (as high prices encourage people to purchase a commodity as it is perceived as being of high quality) however scarcity does not necessarily correspond to price, a commodity can be scarce and worthless, its value must be located elsewhere [381]. As Perelman suggests, economists have also confused a 'metaphysical' value or rather a continuum between religious, family and economic values but coterminous with this, the market system tends to devastate anything that has a price label, such as air or water [382]. Perelman compares the concept of value to that of gravity suggesting that the relationships between firms and households hold the economy in balance, just as physical bodies at a distance hold the planets of the solar system in balance [383]. John Stuart Mill stated, "[a]lmost every speculation respecting the economic interests of a society thus constituted, implies some theory of Value: the smallest error on that subject infects with corresponding error all our other conclusions; and anything vague or misty in our conception of it, creates confusion and uncertainty in everything else." [384]. Furthermore, the more permanent an investment is, the more uncertainty pervades the decision making process in its development, but what if some of this uncertainty resulted from an inability to read or measure intangible benefits? Physical theories built around conservation laws, such as the conservation of matter and the conservation of energy, typically are thought to influence economics, however, as a description of economic relations they have very little explanatory power (rather they can be understood as imitational factors of supply and demand within physical space and time)? [385]. Economies operate in something not quite like the Newtonian world because the concept of value can vary wildly. For example, economists may use scalar dimensions because in production the lapse of time is a negative intangible.

An economists' understanding of both physics and metaphysics may account for why speculation itself is both rational and irrational. However, intangible assets both do and do not operate in a scalar Newtonian world. Thus, there *have* been successes in the measurement of intangible effects in the market place. If the prediction is successful and the market moves one way so profitability make up for losses, but presumably the predictive ambit may apply at one time only in a limited area, so may only be a partial account for catallaxy, or for areas of specialisation and their complex relationship with growth [386]. The complexity is compounded in the measurement of intangible assets throughout the myriad *potential* intangible accountables of the economy.

'Floating value', is economic value given in the application of regulation but Perelman points out there are no discount rates in the natural sciences, whilst business may value natural resources as no different from paper value, clearly there is a qualitative difference. For example, money is a 'manufactured resource', only useful where recognized [387]. Perelman points to the economist Arthur Cecil Pigou who suggested that people 'distribute their resources between the present, the near future, and the remote future on the basis of a wholly irrational preference, present, near future, remote future relative to one another, but business has 'no reason at all to consider a lower discount rate for the more distant future.' [388]. Lionel Robbins observed in influential study of economic methodology, economy is a 'complex of 'scarcity relationships.' [389]. Deviation from marginal pricing causes inefficiency and social loss. Furthermore, emotion and intuition exercise more influence in most economic exchanges than abstract or outright knowledge. Most economists might recognise that it cannot be assumed that: Firstly, everybody behaves in a rational manner, or, secondly, that everyone's idea of rational behaviour is the same.

Intangible Assets, Real Options and Risk

Berk, Green and Naik (1998 and 1999) show that Research and Development projects and new ventures display high level of systematic risk, and Ho, Xu and Yap (2003) empirically demonstrate that Research and Development investment increase a firm's systematic risk [390]. Wyatt (2002) remarks that the risk associated to Intangible Assets (IAs) is higher than risk associated to tangible assets, since generally Intangible assets precede investment in tangible assets [391]. Therefore, investment in Intangible assets is characterised by uncertainty. As Marzo points out risks reduce during investment, is high in researching and reaches a lower level at marketing phase [392]. The arrival of new information and knowledge make reduction of risk possible during the life of an investment in an intangible asset [393]. It follows then that Intangible assets are far from being value-free. However, significant growth can arise from investment in Intangible assets. Furthermore, risk reduction can itself be an Intangible asset. For any given project, a reduction of the value of the real option is positively correlated to the risk variance of the underlying asset value [394].

Table 4. Showing types of intangibles and risk mitigation

Positive Intangibles	Negative Intangibles	Remediation of Intangible threats
Human capital (knowledge) Organisational capital (Collective knowledge, policies, regulations) Information capital (Intellectual property, patents) Market Positioning Statutory based Customer based Market based Contract based Technology based Social capital Bonding capital Bridging capital	Threat of substitute products and services New market entrants Switching costs Slack (time lost) Barrier to entry Obligations Complaints Unknown unknowns Threats to supply Barriers to research and development Product differentiation Planning	Environmental scanning Regulation Education Market capture Rights Networking Known unknowns Fulfilment of terms Patents Motivators

Economic Intangibles are 'non rival' assets. They are assets that one cannot see or touch, such as patents and goodwill, but become relevant when subject of a market transaction or even a potential transaction. They offer future benefits or detriments without physical embodiment. The rationale for focus on Intangible assets follows from relative inability of economic forecast to predict turning points in economic behaviors. If economic use is equivalent to diminished consumption, what if, as well as devaluation, new modes of economy lead to aspects of consumption based on concepts of the 'yet to be seen' or 'exploited'? The point is not simply the transposition of psychological needs wants and desires with economic rationale, rather that intangible assets both affect economic behavior and enhance the value of capital assets. The economic measurement of intangibles involves the complex interaction between people, goods, services, aspirations (needs, wants, desires) and qualities of capital, which have yet to be measured in generally accepted intangible principles [395].

Critical mass as well as a perception of intangibility or little need are sometimes put forward as reasons why organizations neglect to manage their reputations. However, increasingly intangible assets are something that can be measured. As Doorley and Garcia (2015) point out, reputation has a liability factor – so Public Relations strategists monitor, measure and make plans for managing reputation assets and make contingencies for vulnerabilities and crises [396]. Well known measures include the *Harris-Fombrun Reputation Quotient,* which evaluates reputation among multiple audiences, according to 20 characteristics of reputation dimensions. Among which are organizational fundamentals – service and products, finance, environment, the brand appeal and emotional resonance, leadership and social responsibility among them [397]. The efficacy of particular campaigns can be assessed through population sampling among the stakeholder audience, surveying key publics, and monitoring customer feedback, stakeholder interaction, and even measures such as organizational mood, and leadership consultation.

Chapter 11

'An Endless Instance': Making Meaning in Mediated Messages

'It is always a risk to speak to the press: they are likely to report what you say' – Hubert H. Humphrey

There is a day in mid-March 2013 when North Korea disappeared from the Internet [398]. The background to this 'pseudo-event' was the continuing North Korean rhetoric about nuclear arms, a build-up of diplomatic tension in Asia and military tension along the South Korean border. On May 13 news reports about North Korea were minimal, press reports were minimal, and on May 14 the only visible information about the presence of North Korea on the Internet was a short piece from the Japanese press saying a diplomat had been sent to North Korea but that the Japanese Government no longer knew where he was [399]. Even the satellite imagery of North Korea on the Internet showed an area with no light, but surrounding South Korea and China as comparatively luminescent, attributable to the lack of power infrastructure development. Two days later the Korean leader reappeared on national television but the apparent North Korean belligerence had eased in the Western media [400].

In its media effect the disappearance of North Korea for one day from the Internet in mid-May 2013 is a 'staged event' belonging to a particular kind of conditioned media logic which has reference to the predominant modes of news coverage, in which familiar formats introduce certain categories of event or 'non-event' [401]. This event is so-called 'anti-noise' in mass media hype. It is noisy precisely because of its deafening silence, because as consumers of Internet news items we pay next-to-nothing to hear nothing about the status of North Korea in one day mid-May – we have over-invested in its nothingness – either the Korean leader would re-emerge in the public eye and life would go on as normal in late May 2013, or it wouldn't. In the event life went on 'almost as normal,' in North Korea and the disruption to the North Korean internet was short-lived in 2013. However, it was repeated on 22 December 2014 [402], as reported in both the New York Times and by the BBC the following day. The BBC pointed out that the tech-savvy North Koreans are proliferate mobile phone users (1 in 12 of the population) but that many of its peoples are blocked from using the World-Wide-Web. North Korean's can access 'innocuous topics' [403] but cannot access websites outside North Korea. Only the trusted elite, commercial and military agents have such access. Nevertheless, such access as there was in the North Korean system was brought down in 2013 and again 2014 probably by cyber-attack, not that any government has claimed responsibility. The only route for internet into North Korea is via China but sources argue the message of internet disruption might be one of temporary geopolitical 'vulnerability.'

This chapter comments on the contemporary manifestations and implications of mass media hype in the Internet age, with a particular application to conditions of post-industrial journalism. Newsworthy events can take on the characteristics of a 'long-tail' with a global distribution. Such a 'long-tail' of media hyper-activity can occlude 'secondary effects' including aporias in representation and media presence online. In this context, concepts of censorship, cultivation, pseudo-event, and fake-news, remain as relevant as ever, despite – and perhaps even more so because of the proliferation of available information in post-industrial journalism. While the chapter affirms that there are advantages in the digitalisation of media in the post-industrial era, issues of gate keeping can be seen to be compromised in aspects of content dissemination, audience interpretation and media availability, so Public Relations practitioners should always plan to have more than one pathway to disseminate their message.

Mass media communication is the transmission of signal usually from a single source to a large audience. A media such as Television, radio, (e) book or (e) newspaper or Internet, transmits it. Social media is a form of active participant (one to one; one to many) networked mass media. Such a communication tool is ubiquitous in the developed world, giving rise to the 'knowledge society' and liberating vast amounts of information for education and entertainment but it is not without 'side-effects.' The concept of the media creation of the 'mean world' perception among audiences and possible intergenerational influence have meant that the uses and effects of media are at best ambiguous, normally only fleetingly uplifting, and often seen as divisive or diversionary. The term 'mean world syndrome' was invented by George Gerbner [404] and describes a phenomenon in which the violence of mass media content makes the audience perceive the world to be more adverse than it is, it is a form of 'confirmation bias.' There are no such things as 'neutral' mass media. Increasingly the global reach of mass media – television, radio, some forms of Internet – has meant that newsworthy events have a long tail; the portion of a large audience of reception that is distant from the head or central part of the story. Within this context the phenomenon of mass media hype, or intensified and exaggerated publicity in the media over an issue is characterised by the magnitude and intensity of the coverage of a particular issue and may produce complex and undifferentiated intended and unintended effects. But as Susan Orlean noted: 'Brave' is one of those words that has been bleached of most of its meaning these days, thanks to far too many appearances in the glaring light of ad slogans and corporate Public Relations. I never thought about anything as brave anymore; it just seemed like a flabby, glib cliché." Such effects may include aporias and occlusions in representation, which may or may not obscure issues of real-world urgency. The long tail produced by media hype can hide unintended or even 'camouflaged' issues; it can point to absences that are generated in response to media hype, or to the cessation of familiar media content over the short term. Through the 'long-tail' effect of audience perception (or more precisely the divergence of initial trigger issue and the later incidents of narration and the manner of their cessation), the gatekeeping mechanism of 'newsworthiness' may be compromised.

AUDIENCE CULTIVATION

The cultivation of audiences by the mass media leads to the suspension or endorsement of certain representations of heuristic and peripheral information processing. The sensationalism of media, scaremongering, the bad-world syndrome, may serve to condition media watchers and consumers into feelings of helplessness, information between parties and the possibilities for non-optimisation of its use. This metaphor is also relevant for an open society in as much as citizen journalism while accentuating the 'immediacy' of reporting lacks editorial consistency and is 'subjective, 'leading to 'information decay' because of the lack of contextual corroboration. For example, some forms of social media can mirror news items produced from commercial news outlets, while generating little in themselves that is newsworthy, obscuring rather than verifying information that has previously had editorial context. On the other hand, media can also be seen as a force of enlightenment, supplementing forms of education and contributing to progress by disseminating ideas and information, providing enjoyment and exposing political corruption [405]. As Jeff Domansky notes: "*When it comes to blogging, news releases, news stories, or most other content, I hope you get the idea that the only thing more important than the deadline is the headline!*"

The ratio of censored items (understood as being news items that do not receive balanced perspective or coverage) and 'pseudo-event' will be higher in post-industrial journalism because of the loosening of the gatekeeping effect of editorial verification that has ensued with the rise of social media and citizen-journalism and the increasingly decentralisation and mobility of news reporting. This can be measured by examining the relationship between the publics' comprehensibility of an issue in relation to its media sources, and comparing and contrasting the understanding of an issue in relation to its media source.

MEDIA CONDITIONS

Thus while it could be said that the mass media are characterised by an undifferentiated aggregate of disordered and sometimes darkly reflective images of mass society [406], media themselves rely upon many effects that are both sensory and narrational, including devices of communication medium usage such as spectacle, simplification, and exaggeration. Furthermore, media are forms of meta-information – they are part of the power and socioeconomic system that they report on, and as media are themselves formed by series of words and images, stories, rhetoric and sensory impressions all intended to gain attention and influence. Indeed, the concept of truth may itself be 'mediated,' that is represented, disguised or limited in various ways, particularly under conditions of censorship. Although the logic of the market should dictate that information can be updated and corroborated by new and better information, in fact the relationship between veracity and information decay is not as well understood in the era of post-industrial journalism is it was under centralised news dissemination, due to the exponential increase in the manufacture of digital information data. (In 2007 for the first time more digital data was created than storage in which to host it – estimated at approximately 264 Exabyte's, [407] for example). Furthermore, the proliferation of Television and radio channels in the satellite, cable and broadband era has brought a plethora of information alternatives, increased mobility and decentralisation of media reporting, but as Bernstein [408] suggests, not necessarily "better information …[rather] increased quantity of information ... without any consistent improvement in quality." This is turn may lead to 'degraded' time, decision-making and investment decisions [409]. It is also apparent that we are in an era of 'post-industrial' journalism in which proximity to the medium of news transmission is, with mobile communication technologies, no-longer of over-riding concern [410]. This has added new editing challenged exacerbated by citizen journalism that is proliferated within social media dissemination. As Henry Kissinger once put it: “Does anyone have any questions for my answers?”

As far as audience reception and consumption are concerned, information needs to be paid for in some way (by act of transfer) and there is also an opportunity cost in deciphering it both in a business sense (acting on business intelligence) and in a semantic sense (involving the creation of meaning or the maintenance of a worldview) [411]. There is also a trade-off between the time needed to digest information and the incremental benefit derived from it [412]; thus, the effort involved in sorting out sense from nonsense has to compete with the stimulatory pleasure of the next burst of mediated information perceived. From the perspective of information release, a ‘long-tail’ of media hype might be expected to taper once the newsworthiness of an item becomes less critical -- taper but not cease altogether, and certainly not along with the medium of dissemination! The basic concepts (purpose and theories) of mass communication have stayed valid (including theories with modifications for social media influence) from the days of newsprint into today’s digital media world; bridging both print and digital (electronic) formats. However, mass media has become more interactive, and the original concept of a widespread one-way communication has given way to a one-to-many-to-many-one model in the era of citizen journalism and social media.

IMPLICATIONS

As Boorstin has observed, those who relate the news, the reporters, need to differentiate between events and pseudo-events [413] as much as do news consumers. However, there are also sequences of events presented in patterns, so-called ‘pseudo-pattern-events,’ which are newsworthy stages of hyped mass-media productions made to resemble events, or newsworthy events presented in sequence so as to create the effect of a causal link. In mass media hype then there is a feeling of inflating of events and an ambiguity about "covering vs. creating and about cause vs. impact" [414]. Media hype also has a tendency to "transform single cases to general social problems and mobilize social outrage" even when that outrage is inspired by a lack of knowledge [415]. However, the trigger event and the chain of narrative incidents may diverge in the 'longtail' of audience reception.

Consequently, in instances of mass media hype (particularly when audiences are looking for a news item which has not yet been aired) the perception that the news item is the result of someone else's systematic reasoning about a problem [416] is temporarily suspended, the cue and the cognitive effort are disproportional – gatekeeping trust is swept aside. Occlusions are then more or less obvious, because the long tail has signalled the rise in newsworthiness and its sudden absence is noteworthy (where it might not have been to such an extent in asynchronous print-based sources). Post-industrial journalism might correspondingly 'prime' its audiences for pro-longed anxiety over un-reported items.

A related phenomenon in current practices of media censorship (on a continuum with de-representation) is a 'sound-bite.' A 'sound bite' is a short phrase or sentence that captures the essence of a speech or message. The term was popularised in the 1970s amongst political campaigns. It is a short clip of speech or music taken from a longer piece, and standing in the place of a longer segment in a news media item. 'Sound bites' are controversial in journalism ethics because if the context of a 'sound bite' is not clearly defined its meaning can be misleading or confusing. Sound-bit editing, whereby selected contextual elements are censored, cropped (reduced in size or subedited), or dropped altogether from a media item, which has the result of foregrounding only specific (often emotive and sensationalised) comments without description of their background. As Bob Schieffer notes: "[i]n so many of the other beats these days, there are these layers of Public Relations people that you have to go through to get to the newsmakers themselves."

This is a relatively new phenomenon because of digitalisation of news media. While it may be part of the "magnifying impact" digitalization has upon structural imbalances in the production, circulation, and accessibility of information" [417] it is a form of unethical practice which has adverse effects on audiences' perceptions of the value or importance of media news items. Sound-bite journalism is sensationalist, and may spread misperceptions of alarm and relativize the truth-value of media items, destabilising knowledge and perspective on current newsworthy events. This is part of the concept of information overload, which is a symptom of the proliferation of information sources and a pace of reception beyond processing time, and may result in the decontextualisation of information from its source – a tweet of a 140 digital characters may not contain a thorough story, for example. As such, media in whatever channel (online, radio or Television) are providing not just an economy of symbols but also conditioning of social behaviour.

While there may be value in applying value judgments to media items, about weather irregularities due to climate change, for example, for educational purposes, and thereby eliciting a response to climate change issues, this value can be eroded if the media item is inaccurate, de-contextualised or forces wildly interpretative meaning construal's. As Alvin Adams notes: "[m]y view is different. Public Relations are a key component of any operation in this day of instant communications and rightly inquisitive citizens." Perhaps this is also related to Ramonet's [418] assertion that 'seeing is understanding,' meaning the mediated society that consumes images blames the receiver of information for practising the choice of interpretation, as he or she can become meaningfully informed on his or her own. Increasingly, either by subsuming within a media conglomerate or by the immediacy (but also the subjectivity) of citizen-journalism, security in the accessibility, reliability and credibility of journalistic information can be brought into question. A media outlet may rush to publication (in a print or digital medium) with a story based on partial or incomplete information from a tweet. Although interactivity and collaboration have increased in some areas of the global information network and there are more mechanisms for open social participation, this generally has not led to an improvement in the quality of information available. Whilst one can argue that the media plays a role in maintaining "vital links and connections necessary for a cohesive social order" it does so without much thought to the effect in any localised sense, (much as water will flow down a hill instead of up it) [419]. In addition, although giant media conglomerates, dominate the market and culture of media (such as the Murdoch Group, AOL-Time Warner, Microsoft and Google) deregulation has weakened the objectivity of the media and its relation to truth-value (through an accentuation of multiple 'subjectivities' of mobile and citizen journalism).

Consequently, the era of the citizen journalist adds further challenges to the assigned professional role of the journalist in any democracy. The importance of state sovereignty as an arbitrator in a version of 'truth' which the nation affirms cannot be underestimated if not from an economic perspective but a scientific one in the preservation of agreed standard(s) of truth-value and ethical reporting. As Garcia de Madariaga [420] states, "the objectivity and the role of the media as monitors of power are less valuable in a society which is increasingly subject to the dictates of commercial rationality and which turns most journalists into mere disseminators of consent" [421]. On the other hand, the relationship of the media with systems of 'power' is less than clear-cut – truth-value and objectivity tend to transcend their sources. It is also humbling to note that despite the increased vaunting of knowledge and progress brought about by the advances of technology and the informed society, only about one-sixth of the world's population have 'access' to this network [422]. Thus, not only does it become an issue of the have and have nots (of access and/or ownership); of connectivity with developed technology, but also the epistemological issues of using information to give people knowledge -- the relevancy of news information is also of geopolitical importance -- its announcements and its absences. As Richard P. Feynman notes: "Reality must take precedence over Public Relations, for nature cannot be fooled."

'Alternative Facts' in Global Public Relations

As Abraham Lincoln suggested, "character is like a tree and reputation like its shadow. The shadow is what we think of it; the tree is the real thing" [423]. A truism of reputation management is that communication cannot make a bad product good and it is all too easy to confuse behaviour and performance with communication. Therefore, while common objectives should be coordinated with business objectives, they are distinct from them [424]. Furthermore, systems are dynamic – human communication is a form of 'open system'. The individual is both shaped by environments and a shaper of environments. Thus as, Doorley and Garcia (2011) state, "the challenge of professional Public Relations is dealing with truth, falsity and ambiguity, and managing through the muddle with integrity" [425]. Therefore, the integrity of a Public Relations practitioner is premised on the extent to which he or she can exercise professional judgment and promote statements that are true and beneficial to the client [426].

In today's globalised market Public Relations involves new technologies such as satellite, optical fibre and the internet and also involves the active role of business and the globalisation of opportunities and challenges to business [427]. The McLuhan 'global village' characterised by convergence and divergence is very much a realisable experience. Divergence involves the retention of the uniqueness of individual societies confronting globalisation. Without originality, globalisation and the political and economic domination over non-industrial countries or homogenisation of industrialised countries are assured [428]. However, cosmopolitan peoples follow a particular strand of internationalism, which advocates a universal humanism. This 'between-and-across-nation' identity transcends regional particularism. For the cosmopolitan in today's world, multinational employees, investors and customers, satellite TV, foreign governments, international organisations, the World Trade Organisation, the World Bank and international Non-Governmental Organisations, all figure as stakeholders in a global diaspora; an identity formed from amalgam of other identities.

Communications about globalisation are propositions about society [429] and convey a description of society's current state, fulfilling the systems' need for self-knowledge. The global and local refer to different sizes or ranges, a global value indicates perspective or frame and local value indicates perspective or frame from the point of view of globalisation. The system exists as the reality it observes, or the system constructs reality as it constructs itself [430]. There are thought to be four types of communities – those that are closed to each other, single communities, autonomous political units, and those that are globalised and inter-connected in scale and scope. For Hardt, (1979) ". . . [t]he study of mass communication can make sense only in the context of a theory of society; thus questions of freedom and control of expression, of private and public spheres of communication and of a democratic system of mass communication must be raised as part of an attempt to define the position of individuals in contemporary industrialised western societies" [431]. Through the effects of globalisation, there is a complex diffusion of ideas, information, capital and people across national boundaries. These may entangle local and global entities and identities – in multiple possibilities. As Pal and Dutta (2008) suggest, with the "disappearance of time and space as materialised and tangible dimension to social life" [432]. It is necessary for Public Relations practitioners to communicate quickly, accurately and with empathy among a Public Relations proliferation of stakeholder groups. In a globalised world, there is a fragmented hyperactive network of communication and information flow, which characterises the interplay of power and controls transnational relationships. Public Relations practitioners and theoreticians of Public Relations need to be sensitive to the entwined flows of identities, ethnicities, information, technologies, media, commodities that articulate the roles of power, structure, agencies in dynamic rhetorical relationships, which are distributed in and among, ethnicities, info-scapes, technologies, the media and commodities in the transnational cultural milieu [433]. However, they cannot pre-suppose a common audience, or an audience of all one type or education. 'Alternative facts,' take their place in a post-modern world in which everything is increasingly seen in terms of everything else, horizontal hierarchies proliferate over vertical hierarchies. However, information can be acted which preserves some hierarchies over others.

Mass media hype and alternative facts (so-called 'fake news') can produce anxiety in the audience because of the dissonance between versions of truth and perceptions of reality. In such situations, avoiding panic is important. Aside from perception checking – observing others, asking questions, interacting it takes a conscious effort to avoid panicking which is an over-reaction to a real or imagined problem. Emotional panic can shutdown conscious thoughts and feelings, producing an effect akin to shock in which a person cannot think clearly of make decisions, making it difficult to retain information. Panic is a natural reaction that can become prolonged. If it is produced, it can create exaggeration of a problem, temporary 'paralysis of thought and action' and dysfunctionality. So try to stay calm. Remind yourself that panic can be reduced by:

- Learning to recognise the signs
- Take deep breaths
- Try to find what you are afraid of.
- Check facts, check perceptions
- Make a decision to take responsibility and tackle fear
- Make a positive outcome [434].

Although fear and anxiety are a natural response to threat perceived or real; they are usually associated with a problem in the future, but last for a short time and the acute sensation of discomfort passes. When the discomforting situation lasts longer, people can be stuck. One obvious coping mechanism is to avoid situations that make them anxious. When experiencing anxiety or sensing fear, the body prepares for flight or flight. However, in most first world countries it is also apparent that people no longer face same kinds of threats today as formerly in hunter-gatherer societies, for example, most of the time. However, when they do, in order to suppress, panic, fear and phobias, the following behaviours are recommended:

- Avoid situations that makes you afraid
- Know yourself
- Try to learn more about the fear or anxiety
- Exercise
- Relax
- Healthy eating
- Avoid alcohol, or drink in moderation
- Faith

So if the news events make you overly anxious contextualise them by asking in what ways and how do they affect me right now? Ask yourself are my feelings appropriate to the reality of my current situation? As a Public Relations practitioner, you will need to keep a cool head! The storm will eventually blow over!

Chapter 12

'JOINING THE DOTS': NETWORKING SKILLS IN PUBLIC RELATIONS

'There is only one thing in the world worse than being talked about, and that is not being talked about' – Oscar Wilde

You are in the middle of a busy report that you are writing for your boss that makes use of some analytic data that can sustain more than one interpretation. You are wondering which interpretative scenario is the preferred one, the option that shows where the data could lead in the future or the more conservative option adopt, that shows where it is now. You cast your eyes around your colleagues to see who you could ask who might help you. Seeing no one who is immediately available, your recall the colleagues you know in other similar organisations. You look at the web of network connections you have on social media. In twenty seconds, your pool of colleagues to consult has started from a handful and grown to many!

In any working environment, it is important to **stay in touch** with peers, mentors, supervisors, managers, colleagues, customers. In any business environment knowing who your clients are and whom you can contact for advice, resources, or assistance whenever necessary is an important part of on-the-job knowledge. Aside from the business alliances that organisations may themselves form, it is essential that individuals form networking capabilities that may enhance the social and professional contexts in which they work. A social network is a social structure characterised by a variety of social ties between agents and actors. In today's everyday working environment characterised by predominant use of information and computer technologies, social networking sites (or online platforms that facilitate and build social networks among people – for example, *Facebook, Myspace, Bebop, delicious, LinkedIn, Fledge Wing, Spaces, Xing, Yammer, Instagram, Snapchat)* make internet-based user profiles sharable, adaptable and interlinked allowing users to share ideas, activities, interests, events and expertise. Consequently, by using such online community services people are able to extend the range of their social networks over a greater geographical area more quickly than ever before and across time. This gives virtual credence to the concept of the 'global village'. The characteristics of social 'technographics' reveals that people can be grouped largely into any one or combination of six profile activities. These are creators, critics, collectors, joiners, spectators, and inactives [435]. These roles are assumed by both everyday participants and by academic members of online social networking media.

A tension exists in the modern workplace between the considerable amount of time that people may spend in relative isolation engaged in activities which require space and time for individual concentration, and the need to interact with a community of stakeholders, the need to confer and consult with professional peers and colleagues to share ideas and to validate and critique each other's work. Consequently, Public Relations practitioners must frequently shift between varying levels of social engagement from seclusion to the intensity of constant interaction with large audiences of people. Networking is essential for peer validation and support. As Benkler (2006) states, "[w]e are a networked society now – networked individuals connected with each other in a mesh of loosely knit, overlapping, flat connections . . . we see social norms and software coevolving to offer new, more stable, and richer contexts for forging new relationships . . . these do not displace older relations" [436]. This chapter will examine the origins of the workplace-networking concept and explore its applicability to the Public Relations context.

Table 5. Showing advantages and disadvantages of social networking sites

Advantages of social networking sites	Disadvantages of social networking sites
Allow people to stay in touch (with relatives, friends, business associates, class-mates) despite barriers of geographical locations	Personal information such as email address, location and age, can be misused
Permits interactivity and sharing of information (messages, files, photos, videos)	The creation of fake profiles for fraudulent purposes is possible – real identities can be difficult to find
Allows for the expansion of association of contacts, interaction permits association of thoughts and interests	Lack of site regulation can lead to online harassment and misuse
Facilitates an easier and faster way of collecting information	Social media cannot convey paraverbal information about communicants
Because of extensive and expanding networks, social media can be used for promoting business, products and websites	Social media can distract attention away from more formal job related tasks

As Grieco and Hosking (1987) state there is a sense in which networks "recruit employers" in building knowledge bases of companies and jobs [437]. In the contemporary workplace, networks can provide knowledge of firstly, a variety of places of employment and employers; secondly, job prospects for redundancies and recruitment drives; thirdly, the requirements of jobs and; fourthly movements of network members from one place of employment to another. Networks give people a shared sense of order and a shared sense of social identity [438]. Furthermore, networks combine three inter-related factors. Firstly, they **instil values** that are held in common and help to promote organisational identity and shared goals, they help to reinforce stable understandings concerning activities and relationships, conditions of interaction and exchange and threats to values, that coalesce around clients goals and organisational identity – issues that concern the Public Relations practitioner [439].

As Bianchi (2012) argues, networking is described as an "apparatus for contemporary subjectification processes" [440]. The most popular of the networking sites in today's information age are the online social networking services such as *Facebook, Orkut, Twitter, Linked-In, MySpace,* these are used by up to 47% of American adults, for example [441] which link people and their communications in virtual creative spaces, that are bounded, discrete and rationalised. As Donde, Chopped and Ranjith (2012) suggest, "a social networking service is an online service which provides a platform for building social network or social relations among people" [442]. In essence, a social networking site is an online community of internet users.

Donde, Chopped and Ranjith (2012) suggest that there is an inverse relationship between age and going online. In many developed parts of the world generation y and z have high-speed internet access at home, are users of text messaging, social networking sites, instant messaging, they read and create blogs and download music [443]. Social networking sites are increasingly the subject of commentary and debate within education. One the one hand, as Brown and Dugoid (2000) have suggested, ". . . despite the buzz about on-line learning and communities, it can be difficult to form suitably dense communities to support learning in cyberspace" [444], on the other, the 'digital highway' opens up the possibility of distance education to thousands of geographically dispersed and potentially socially distal students. There are two sides to the argument – some educationalists regard social networking as potentially expanding the engagement of learners with their studies, or Public Relations practitioners with their clients others regard social networking as potentially a threat to traditional means of communication [445]. You might not be able to convey every nuance to someone online, that you could in a face-to-face meeting, and after all as Arik Hansen says "*If I had to make a generalization, I'd say PR people are typically "people pleasers." That means we want to make our clients happy – no matter the cost."* That face-to-face meeting alongside the social media chatting could be well worthwhile.

As Todd, Harris, Harries and Wheeler (2009) suggest, there are four categories of career success – human capital, organisational sponsorship, socio-demographic status and stable individual differences [446]. These may interact through different stages within the span of a given career (as diachronic influences that may be changeable) or they affect synchronically in the course of the employer or employees engagement with the workplace. Political skill is thus a component of any social media activity and is defined as ". . . the ability to effectively understand others at work and to use such knowledge to influence others to cat in ways that enhance one's personal or organisational objectives [447]. According to Todd et al., (2009) politically skilled individuals' exhibit three characteristics – they excel in networking, demonstrate sincerity, have interpersonal influence and are socially astute [448]. Furthermore, political skills may influence ability to handle and manage workloads including role overload, leadership effectiveness, team performance, and the relationship between overload and strain [449].

Scholars of career success define good performance as ". . . the sum of accumulated positive psychological experience one gathers as a result of work". There are both subjective and objective measures of career success. Objective measures include salary and promotions and subjective measures are both career and life satisfaction [450]. However, success is something to be shared and not wholly owned as Sandi Young notes, "*[t]oday's consumer doesn't need to own. Why own when you can share, and increase cost efficiencies at the same time?"* hence part of a networker's role is to know when and how to share with others – the 'tipping point' – that makes an interaction optimistic, and worthwhile. Fortunately, the ubiquitous mobile and social media makes the sharing of such moments both more possible and more enjoyable.

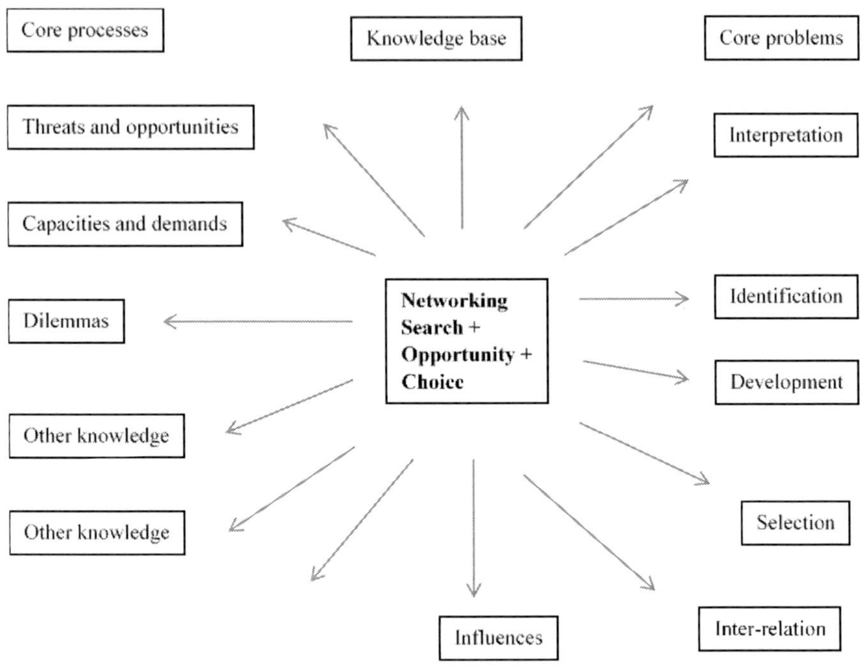

Figure 3. Showing networking values and skills [451].

Organisations are political in nature and in order to be successful social skills are vitally important. Political skills involve the ability to understand others at work to use knowledge to influence others [452], to read situational requirements and alter social presentation in ways that affect others and to develop diverse networks of people that use for personal gain. Some aspects of political skill are dispositional in nature (involving interpersonal influence) and other dimensions (such as networking ability) can be developed and learned to enable an individual to better cope with work environment [453]. Sometimes a Public Relations practitioner will want to an influence a person by talking with them and exchanging views at other times, he or she will want to share material with another to create a favourable reaction. As Melanie Taylor puts it: "*If you care about something, you'll share it with others. Just by viewing, liking, and sharing friends' videos, you become part of the story. It's challenging for brands to reproduce such an emotional experience, but to get this kind of traction is essential.*" Therefore, Public Relations practitioners may also be good at putting people at ease, and at starting and maintaining conversations with people. Sometimes a Public Relations practitioner or reputation manager will be a networker, sometimes a negotiator, sometimes a lobbyist but always a persuader and one who can exercise political skill in the sense of rhetorical capability and positional conversation. Political skill involves social effectiveness and understanding of workplace interactions [454], this is a variable that equips those individuals who are high it to better understand interactions and social outcomes in the workplace. Doorley and Garcia recommend six principles in community relations in networking:

- Be involved and committed
- Treat everyone fairly, build reputation one relationship at a time
- Be strategic
- Be forward focused
- Embrace diversity
- If things go wrong, make the right quickly [455].

Political skill consists of cognitive and behavioural components that allows employees to balance both in acceptable manner [456]. Employees high in political skill seen as better performers compared with those low in political skills [457]. Political skill also influences subjective career success. Individuals fill gap between control they possess and the control they desire. Under the personal control model, employees desire more control over relation between socialisation tactics of the firm and seeing themselves and their role in a positive light to achieve state of homeostasis between the perception of themselves and their role in the organisation [458]. The social influence theory [459] leads us to believe that political skill will be positively associated with perceptions of being marketable outside the organisation [460]. Evaluation measures for the social influences of behaviours include: the level of cognitive processing, perceived intentionality, relative social status, and direction of change [461]. Todd et al. (2009) also identify four dimensions of political skill – networking ability, interpersonal influence, social astuteness and sincerity [462]. Getting your clients views across may more important than the brand awareness brought by advertising but a Public Relations practitioner might combine by interacting in ways that are congruent with the stakeholders values an satisfy an informational demand that they previously couldn't perceive. As Brittany Bang notes: "*[f]rom the magnificent to the mundane, it seems it's all fair game for social sharing. However, brands cannot focus on the mundane when interrupting consumer conversations online. They need to be incredibly useful resources to be relevant – and to prompt action.*"

As a Public Relations practitioner when you are not advancing the reputation of the brand for the client, you may represent the client in enhancing his or her own reputation within and beyond the organisation. Frame working an interactive virtual or social environment in positive terms to improve the connection between the firm's socialisation networks is sometimes necessary – all power to those guest lists! [463]. However, with the personal control model, employees desire more control over relationship between the socialisation tactics of the organisation and whether they are seen themselves in a positive light [464]. An employee who receives less than optimal career satisfaction might like to seek to incorporate political skills into their repertoire of job-related-skills – influencing others at work and establishing larger networks to change assessment of outcome. A situational antecedent to political skill development may be the effect of technology, for example, an impact of having access to and being involved in instant messaging, virtual worlds and blogging [465]. Thus insights into the wider concerns of management within human resources can inform a Public Relations practitioners toolkit when they actively seek to establish influence over an organisations social network, and to proactively forge new business connections for their clients. Sometimes this can be achieved through virtual interaction, at others in face-to-face meetings and at social events, and sometimes in a combination of each. As Clipson, Wilcon, and DuFrene (2012) state, "social networking via texting, *Facebook*, *Twitter* and similar media is enormously popular with students leads to communication challenges along gender lines" [466]. Men and women use technology differently – *Facebook* (57%) women, 8% more friends and accounting for 62% of sharing. Signs of networking fatigue among young men and some decline in interest among males participating in social networking communities [467]. Generally there are a higher percentage of women spend more time online (76%) than men (70%), typically. But it is difficult to say why this might be the case, whether through social integration or as the result of aggregated task / role functioning, [468]. There are also thought to be differences in social networking usages, for example, between females being sociable and keeping in touch with friends, and male participants invoking peer pressure, and responding as if the online environment was only for advertising or preening! [469]. The effect of social networking is felt and experienced throughout life, including in education, communication, employment, social relationships, and personal productivity [470].

An increasingly popular development in online social networking is the proliferation of applications by third-party companies for use within networks. Of these the most popular and profitable is the category of 'social gaming' in which players perform restricted but frequent actions to build 'resources' within virtual game contexts (for example, *SecondLife*). It is debatable the extent to which such activities encourage entrepreneurship but the rewards system within 'social gaming' has parallels to that in the market place. Micro-blogging sites such as *Twitter* are also popular and allow members to follow coded statements or 'tweets' no longer than 140 characters. As Gail Kelly notes: "[i]n this digital age, there is no place to hide behind Public Relations people. This digital age requires leaders to be visible and authentic and to be able to communicate the decisions they've made and why they've made them, to be able to acknowledge when they've made a mistake and to move forward, to engage in the debate." According to Baron and Markman (2003), an entrepreneur's social skills affect the success of new ventures. They do so by influencing how entrepreneurs' acquire information and relevant resources. As Semrau and Sigmund (2010) state, "Individuals with high networking abilities are highly adept at negotiating, deal making, and conflict management" [471]. Whilst networking ability is an individual-level construct, the reliance of the individual on the network may mean that individuals are constrained by the size of the network relationships. It is also thought that the performance of enterprises, which are more newly established, is more dependent on the size of the network, than enterprises which have been established for a longer time. This is because the network is seen as a resource for financial capital, knowledge and information and because networkers are able to use new relationships [472]. As Norris et al. (2005) suggest, skills involved in networking are related to "interpersonal issues, problem solving, decision-making and managing change" [473]. Characteristics of successful collaboration are "shared vision and objectives, mutual support, effective participation, and appropriate support" [474]. There are also a number of potential barriers, which prevent professionals from working together. These include differences in history, differences in culture and professional norms, rivalry and concerns with status, rewards and responsibilities [475].

Shi, Chen and Zhou (2011) suggest that the roles of political skill dimensions include: networking ability, interpersonal influence, social astuteness and apparent sincerity. These are related to the proactive personality of employees and the role that job performance plays in supervision and altruism [476]. Proactive personality is defined as ". . . the relatively stable tendency to take actions to make environmental change occur" [477]. These changes are more often positive than negative and might include "initiative to effect the environment, to seek out opportunities to improve their situations, to create conditions to improve their social context than those of lower proactive personality" [478]. Furthermore, because networking skills and proactive personality are socially constructed – they are more likely to be a "distal predictor of employees' job behaviours." [479]. Political skill may also be a mediator between pro-active personality and job performance [480]. Katz (1964) observes that employees to carry out specific job requirements and to act beyond what the role requires. Pro-active personalities are prepared to solve problems at work and work socially towards obtaining a better group and inter-personal environment to fulfil their task [481]. In role-performance–behaviours within job descriptions and related to accomplishing the tasks which contribute value to organisation [482]. Extra role performance refers to behaviours aimed at social, psychological and organisational contexts [483]. Altruism is a factor here and in this context refers to the influence of proactive personality on 'extra-role performance' [484]. As Shi et al., (2011) suggest, "[e]mployees high in proactive personality may shape, develop, and exploit their interpersonal relationships actively" [485]. They may also help co-workers with a heavy workload and provide instruction on the new use of technology, which can help free-up resources and enhance productivity [486].

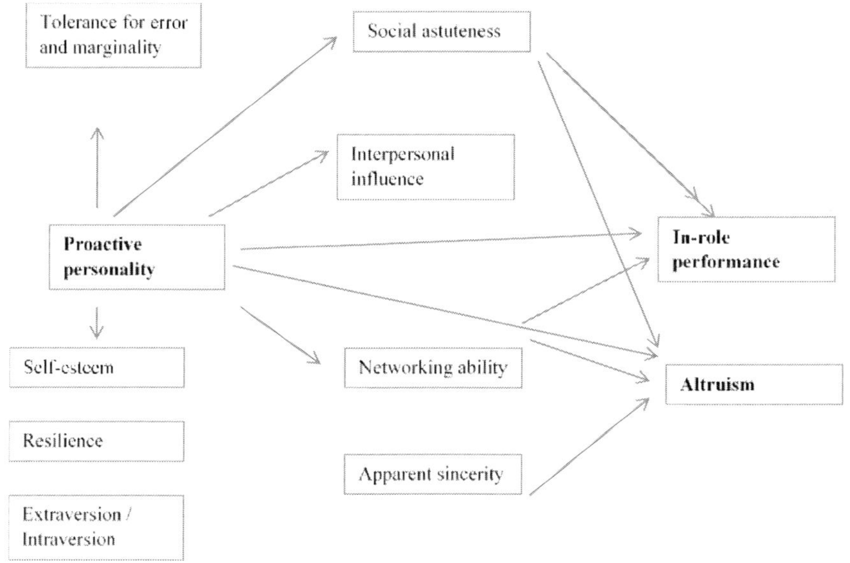

Figure 4. Showing Political Skill Dimensions [487].

Osberg and Maulin (1989) define networking as the "set of strategies . . . used to increase their visibility among interactions with other professionals" [488] and so networking is defined more widely as a "set of strategies used to enhance one's professional visibility" [489]. Hence as Osberg and Maulin (1989) relate visibility acts so as to enhance marketability which in turn promotes career advancement [490]as they put it: "[t]he best way to interest people in your work is to be interested in their work" [491].

A recent development in networking capabilities is the use of 'crowdsourcing'. Crowdsourcing is a specific resource sourcing model in which a 'problem' is presented in an open call to a digital network and allowing the network and a self-organising group work together to find a solution. A related concept is the use of 'cloud computing' which may take place across several different or multiple and many servers over the internet 'Cloud Computing' is a remote computing service which does not have a fixed location but is scalable across potentially thousands of computers. Indeed, cloud computing is a natural extension of the interconnection and inter-operability of information and computer technology and internet users. As Meg Whitman observes: "[w]hat's sort of interesting about the whole Public Relations disaster that is the Net, in some ways, is that the fundamentals are really good." Strom and Strom (2012) identify eleven factors as cautions on the use of electronic social networking sites [492]. These are:

- Don't share personal or private information
- Don't harass or threaten other users
- Don't cyberstalk, spam or send unwanted messages
- Don't insult other races, cultures, genders, sexual life-styles, or religions
- Don't post, transmit, or distribute obscene, sexually explicit, vulgar or pornographic, ethnically offensive, or untrue content
- Don't solicit sexually explicit photos or texts
- Don't post or transmit violent or sexually explicit photographic images of youth
- Don't disrupt the flow of blogs with abuse, repetitive posts, and off-topic content
- Don't impersonate anyone
- Don't steal a password, account data or other information
- Don't post material created by others without permission or organisation

Zofi and Meltzer (2010) regard networking as "really small talk with a target" [493]. It is a critical skill necessary for on-the-job success. Even if you would categorise someone as an effective communicator some areas may also need refinement such as styles of communication, the handling of personality differences, or the persuasion of others [494]. The best advice for networking is the art of turning 'casual conversations into useful connections' [495]. Zofi and Meltzer (2010) also define networking as ". . . the deliberate process of exchanging information, resources, support and access in such a way as to create mutually beneficial alliances for personal and professional success" [496]. It involves building "working relationships with the right people to provide information, support, influence and development" [497]. Other facets of networking involve the creation of environments in which people share resources and experiences, learn from one-another and create positive working relationships [498]. Business networks also may have a personal factor in which close associates, friends and family may share mutual likings and connections, which may be short or long, term in length, as part of stakeholder engagement. Business groups may comprise terms, project partners, committees, councils, even 'unconferences' (informal group discussions within formal arrangements) that share information and resources in order to achieve particular goals. Conole, Galley and Culver (2011) state that groups are defined as being ". . . relatively tightly formed with shared interests and intentions," networks in comparison are a more fluid form of social entity in "which members join, create, and remove themselves through informal and semiformal connections," there is also a third category of networks called collectives "whose networked activities are harvested to generate the 'wisdom of crowds'" [499]. Strategic networks may also be those that form alliances in circumstances of increased complexity and regulation [500].

Okoro (2012) claims that networking members learn better and have better job performance when they work independently and collaboratively and acquire skills of self-discipline as the result of the personal engagements they have through social networking [501]. Okoro (2012) also argues that there is a positive correlation between social networking and student's dedication and interest in acquiring knowledge [502]. However, Kastenmuller et al., (2011) suggest that under conditions of threat, ". . . people shift their priorities from occupational networking towards personal networking" [503].

The Nielsen company reported in 2011 that activity on social networks and blogs occupies more than 13.5 minutes daily (twice that of gaming and 3 times that of email) [504] and furthermore that the top 10 networking sites have some 2.93 billion registered users [505]. Digital interactions were held to have influenced online sales by some 2.2 trillion dollars by 2015 and by 2016, there are believed to be approximately 966 million websites on the internet. 46% of the web traffic between which is from people and 56% from bots. Today, there are approximately 3.4 billion internet users worldwide. Thus, almost half the human population currently use an online medium of some form [506]. In this context, it is pertinent to note that social networking has an influence on both public and private lives. The importance of online social networking sites is growing internationally. Such sites are mobilisers of cultural, human and social capital. They act as swift dissemination sources for the exchange of information and ideas and act as permeable and combinatorial nodes and networks for inter personal and professional association and collaboration. The original vision of the internet inventor Sir Tim Berners-Lee (1999) was for a 'semantic web' in which the networks of collaboration between people and their digital profiles and avatar imprint (for example, likes and dislikes) become analysable by digital machines, and thus peoples' interactions with the internet and the world of information and computer technology become semantically adaptable to their daily lives [507]. Once realised, such a vision would greatly enhance the networking potential of the world-wide-web, between people and people, people and machines, and machines and people. Consequently, social media plays an increasing role in facilitating connections between the agents and allies of the Public Relations practitioner, reaching new audiences, and creating business connections.

REFERENCES

[1] Herman, E. S. and Chomsky, N. (1988). *Manufacturing Consent: The Political Economy of the Mass Media.* New York: Pantheon Books: 306.

[2] Roberts-Bowman, S. (2016) What is Public Relations? In Alison Theaker, (Edit.). *The Public Relations Handbook,* Taylor and Francis: xxvii.

[3] Roberts-Bowman, *ibid.,* xxvii.

[4] Mersham, G., Theunissen, P., and Peart, J. (2009). *Public Relations and Communication Management.* North Shore: Pearson Education New Zealand.

[5] Doorley, J. and Garcia, H. F. (2011). *Reputation Management. The Key to Successful Public Relations and Corporate Communication.* (2nd ed.). New York: Routledge.

[6] Roberts-Bowman, *ibid.,* xxvii.

[7] Sriramesh, K. (2009). Globalisation and Public Relations: The past, present, and the future. *Prism* 6 (2). Retrieved from: http://Public Relationsaxis.massey.ac.nz/publicrelationsism_on-line_journ.html.

[8] McCluhan as cited in Getto E. (2011, July 15).The medium is the message: Celebrating Marshall McLuhan's Legacy. Retrieved from: https://mcluhangalaxy.wordpress.com/2011/07/16/celebrating-marshall-mcluhans-legacy/.

[9] Lincoln cited in Doorley. and Garcia, *ibid.,* 2.

[10] Doorley and Garcia, *ibid.*

[11] Doorley and Garcia, *ibid.,* 38.

[12] Doorley and Garcia, *ibid.*

[13] Lee, S. (2005). The emergence of global public and international Public Relations. *Public Relations Quarterly*, *50*,(2), 14-16.

[14] Lee, *ibid.*

[15] Doorley and Garcia, *ibid.*

[16] Doorley and Garcia, *ibid.*

[17] Doorley and Garcia, *ibid.*

[18] Grunig, James E., et Hunt, Todd. (1984). *Managing Public Relations.* New York: Holt, Rinehart et Winston: 22.

[19] Doorley and Garcia, *ibid.*

[20] Doorley and Garcia, *ibid.*

[21] Doorley and Garcia, *ibid.*

[22] Kearney, M. (1995). The local and the global: The anthropology of globalisation and transnationalism. *Annual Review of Anthropology 24*, 547–565: 548.

[23] Kearney, *ibid.*

[24] Kearney, *ibid.* 551.

[25] Kearney, *ibid.*

[26] Appadurai, A. (1996). *Modernity at Large: Cultural Dimensions of Globalisation.* Minneapolis: University of Minnesota Press.

[27] Kearney, *ibid.*

[28] Guy, J-S. (2009). What is global and what is local? A theoretical discussion around globalization. *The Parsons Journal For Information Mapping*. New York. Retrieved from: http://piim.newschool.edu/journal/issues/2009/02/pdfs/ParsonsJournalForInformationMapping_Guy-JeanSebastian.pdf.

[29] Guy, *ibid.*

[30] Tomlinson, J. (2008). 'Globalisation and Cultural identity'. Retrieved June 17, 2008 from: http://www.polity.co.uk/global/pdf/GTReader2e Tomlinson.pdf, p. 273.

[31] Ihator, A. (2000) Understanding the cultural patterns of the world--An imperative in implementing strategic international Public Relations programs. *Public Relations Quarterly*, *45*(4), 38–44.

[32] Ihator, *ibid.*

[33] Ihator, *ibid.*

[34] Hall, Stuart; T. Jefferson (1976), *Resistance through Rituals, Youth Subcultures in Post-War Britain*. London: Harper Collins Academic: 79.

[35] Lee, S. (2005). The emergence of global public and international Public Relations. *Public Relations Quarterly*, *50*,(2), 14-16.

[36] Hardt, H. (1979) *Social theories of the press*. Beverly Hills, California: Sage Publications. 35.

[37] Pal, M., and Dutta, M. J. (2008). Public Relations in a global context: The relevance ofcritical modernism as a theoretical lens. *Journal of Public Relations Research, 20*(2), 161.

[38] Pal and Dutta, *ibid.*

[39] Dwyer, J. (2009). (4th ed.) *Communication in business: strategies and skills*. Frenchs Forest, N.S.W: Pearson Education Australia.

[40] Mead, G. (2003). Symbolic Interactionism. In E. Griffin, *A first look at communication theory*. (pp. 55-65). New York: McGraw-Hill.

[41] Eisenberg, E. (1984). Ambiguity as strategy in organizational communication. *Communication Monographs*, *51*, 230.

[42] Eisenberg, *ibid.,* 230.

[43] Eisenberg, *ibid.,* 259.

[44] Salazar, A. J. (1996). 'Ambiguity and communication effects on small group decision-making performance'. *Human Communication Research,* 23 (2): 176.

[45] Littlejohn, S. (2002). *Theories of human communication.* Belmont, CA, USA: Wadseworth/Thomson Learning: 158.

[46] Menz, F. (1999). 'What am I gonna do with this? Self-organization, ambiguity and decision-making in a business enterprise'. *Discourse and Society,* 10 (1): 105.

[47] Eisenberg, *ibid.,* 227.

[48] Eisenberg, *ibid.,* 227.

[49] Menz, *ibid.,* 105.

[50] Eisenberg, *ibid.,* 227.

[51] Eisenberg, *ibid.,* 228.

[52] Eisenberg, *ibid.,* 228.
[53] Eisenberg, *ibid.,* 228.
[54] Eisenberg, *ibid.,* 228.
[55] Salazar, *ibid.,* 179.
[56] Salazar, *ibid.,* 178-179.
[57] Eisenberg, *ibid.,* 229.
[58] Eisenberg, *ibid.,* 230.
[59] Eisenberg, *ibid.,* 239.
[60] Eisenberg, *ibid.,* 239.
[61] Tylor, L. (1997). 'Liability means never being able to say you're sorry: Corporate guilt, legal constraints and defensiveness in corporate communication.' *Management Communication Quarterly,* 11 (1): 51-73. 59-60.
[62] Eisenberg, *ibid.,* 231.
[63] Krayer, K. and Bacon, C. (1984). 'Communication ambiguity in job related messages'. *Communication Research Reports,* 1 (1): 88-90.
[64] Pickert, S. M. (1981). 'Ambiguity in referential communication tasks: The influence of logical and social factors'. *The Journal of Psychology,* 109, 51-57.
[65] Pickert, *ibid.,* 62.
[66] Littlejohn, S. (2002). *Theories of Human Communication.* Belmont, CA, USA: Wadsworth/Thomson Learning: 126-127.
[67] Piotrowski, M. V. (2005). *Effective Business Writing. A Guide for those who Write on the Job.* Second Edition. New York: harper Collins Publisher.
[68] DeVito, J. (2012). The self and perception. In *Human communication: The basic course* (12th ed., pp. 50–75). Boston, MA: Pearson: 67.
[69] DeVito, *ibid.,* 68.
[70] Eisenberg, E. (1984). Ambiguity as Strategy in Organizational Communication. *Communication Monographs,* 51: 227-242.
[71] Eisenberg, *ibid.*

[72] Krohn, F. (1994). 'Improving business ethics with the Sapir-Whorf-Korzybski hypothesis in business communication'. *Journal of Education for Business,* 69 (6): 354-359.

[73] Mahin, L. (1998). 'Critical thinking and business ethics'. *Business Communication Quarterly,* 61 (3): 74-78.

[74] Nelson, B. (2003, February 1st). Put their names in lights. *Meetings Net.* Retrieved from: http://meetingsnet.com/corporate-meetings/put-their-names-lights.

[75] Ulmer, R. and Sellnow, T. (2000). 'Consistent questions of ambiguity in organizational crisis communication: jack in the box as a case study'. *Journal of Business Ethics,* 25, 143-155.

[76] Weick, K. E. (1998). 'Enacted sense making in crisis situations'. *Journal of Management Studies,* 27 (4): 305.

[77] Ulmer and Sellnow, *ibid.,* 147.

[78] Cheney, G. (1991). *Rhetoric in an organisational society.* Columbia, SC: University of South Carolina Press.

[79] O'Neill, M. and Kobaynski, S. (2009). 'Risky business: An updated communication perspective'. Competitiveness Review: *An International Business Journal Incorporating Journal of Global Competitiveness,* 13 (1): 645.

[80] O'Neill and Kobaynski, *ibid.,* 645.

[81] Ellsburg, D. (1961). 'Risk, ambiguity and savage axioms'. *Quarterly Journal of Economics,* 75, 643-679.

[82] Hsu, M., Bhatt, M., Adolphs, R., Tranel, D., & Camerer, C. F. (2005). Neural systems responding to degrees of uncertainty in human decision-making. *Science, 310*, 1680–1683.

[83] Risburg, A. (1997). 'Ambiguity and communication in cross-cultural acquisitions: towards a conceptual framework'. Leadership & Organisation Development Journal, 18 (5): 257-266.

[84] Risburg, *ibid.,* 258.

[85] Risburg, *ibid.,* 258.

[86] Amorium, M. (2010). *Ambiguity and the new business normal.* Retrieved from: http://www.maurilioamorium.com/2010/12/ambiguity-and-the-new-business-normal/: 2.

[87] Hooper, D. (2007) Dealing with ambiguity – part 1. Retrieved from: http://www.buildingfutureleaders.com/uploads/4/1/1/4/411493/microsoft_word__dealing_with_ambiguity--part_1.pdf. 1.

[88] Mintzburg, H. (2009). *Managing.* San Francisco: Berrett-Koehler Publishers: 9.

[89] Anthony, S. (2010). 'Grooming leaders to handle ambiguity'. *Harvard Business Review.* Retrieved from: http://blogs.hbr.org/Anthony/2010/07/grooming_leaders_to_handle_ambiguity.html#, para 4.

[90] Anthony, *ibid.,* para 7.

[91] Robbins, S. (1993). *Organizational Behaviour.* Englewood Cliffs, N. J.: Prentice Hall.

[92] Sayers, J. (2005). Managing conflict at work. In F. Sligo & R. Bathurst (Eds.). *Communication in the New Zealand Workplace: Theory and Practice* (pp. 83-94). Wellington: Software Technology New Zealand Ltd.: 83.

[93] Sayers, *ibid.,* 93.

[94] Doorley and Garcia, *ibid.*

[95] Knauer, N. J. (2010). Legal Fictions and Juristic Truth. St. *Thomas Law Review.* 23(1), 1.

[96] Knauer, *ibid.,* 4-5.

[97] Knauer, *ibid.,* 4.

[98] Knauer, *ibid.,* 28.

[99] Knauer, *ibid.,* 50.

[100] Simpson, Z. (2012). The Truths We Tell Ourselves: Foucault on Parrhesia1*Foucault Studies.* Issue 13, 101.

[101] Simpson, *ibid.,* 105.

[102] Simpson, *ibid.,* 108.

[103] Busch, F. (2000). Truth, Lies, Fact, Fiction. *American Scholar.,* 69 (3), 35.

[104] Wojcik, B. (2012). Is Odysseus Cunning. *Filozofia.* 67 (5): 388.

[105] Wojcik, *ibid.,* 397.

[106] Bacon, F. (1934/1601). *The Works of Lord Bacon, With An Introductory Essay And A Portrait. In Two Volumes, Vol. 1.* London: William Ball, Pasternoster Row: 261.

[107] Hollander, J. (1996). The Shadow of a Lie: Poetry, lying and the truth of Fictions. *Social Research: An International Quarterly.* 63 (4), 645.

[108] Hollander, *ibid.,* 648-651.

[109] Hollander, *ibid.,* 659.

[110] Jehlen, M. (2008). *Five Fictions in Search of Truth.* Princeton, New Jersey: Princeton University Press.

[111] Hollander, *ibid.,* 60.

[112] Allen, R. C. (1996). 'Socioeconomic Conditions and Property Crime: A Comprehensive Review and Test of the Professional Literature.' *American Journal of Economic and Sociology,* 55: 293-308.

[113] Stuhring, J. (2011). Unreliability, Deception, and Fictional Facts. *Journal of Literary Theory.* 5 (1), 97.

[114] Ramsden, M. A. (2011). Fictional Frontiers: The Inter-relation of fact and fiction between the world and the text. *Neophilogus,* 95: 342.

[115] Ramsden, *ibid.,* 348.

[116] Ramsden, *ibid.,* 349.

[117] Ramsden, *ibid.,* 351.

[118] Mikkonen, K. (2006). Can Fiction Become Fact? The Fiction-to-Fact Transition in Recent Theories of Fiction. *Style*, 40 (4), 242.

[119] Mikkonen, *ibid.,* 293.

[120] Mikkonen, *ibid.,* 294-295.

[121] Mikkonen, *ibid.,* 302.

[122] Mikkonen, *ibid.,* 302.

[123] Finch, D. Deephouse, D. L., and Varella, P. (2013). Examining and individual's Legitimacy Judgment Using the value – Attitude System: The Role of Environmental and Economic Values and Source Credibility. *Journal of Business Ethics*, 127 (2): 265.

[124] Finch et al., *ibid.,* 265.

[125] Finch et al., *ibid.,* 265.

[126] Finch et al., *ibid.,* 267.

[127] Finch et al., *ibid.,* 267.

[128] Finch et al., *ibid.,* 267.
[129] Finch et al., *ibid.,* 267.
[130] Finch et al., *ibid.,* 268.
[131] Finch et al., *ibid.,* 268.
[132] Finch et al., *ibid.,* 268.
[133] Finch et al., *ibid.,* 268-9.
[134] Flanagin, A. J., Metzger, M. J., Pure, R., Markov, A., and Hartsell, E. (2014). Mitigating risk in ecommerce transactions: perceptions of information credibility and the role of user-generated ratings in product quality and purchase intention. *Electronic Commerce Research*, 14 (1): 1.
[135] Flanagin et al., *ibid.,* 2.
[136] Flanagin et al., *ibid.,* 2.
[137] Flanagin et al., *ibid.,* 2.
[138] Myrden, S. E. and Kelloway, E. K. (2014). Service Guarantees: The Impact of Playing 'Hard to Get' On Perceptions of Firm Credibility and Repurchase Intent. *Journal of Consumer Satisfaction, Dissatisfaction and Complaining Behavior,* 27: 59.
[139] Flanagin et al., *ibid.,* 4.
[140] Flangin et al., *ibid.,* 4.
[141] Myrden and Kelloway, *ibid.,* 55.
[142] Flanagin et al., *ibid.,* 16.
[143] Flanagin et al., *ibid.,* 3.
[144] Flanagin et al., *ibid.,* 3.
[145] Finch, et al., *ibid.,* 269.
[146] Finch, et al., *ibid.,* 270.
[147] Obermiller, C., Ruppert, B., and Atwood, A. (2012). Instructor Credibility Across Disciplines: Identifying Students' Differentiated Expectations of Instructor Behaviors. *Business Communication Quarterly,* 75 (2): 154.
[148] Sabri, O., and Geraldine, M. (2014). When Do Advertising Parodies Hurt? The Power of Humor and Credibility In Viral Spoof Advertisements. *Journal of Advertising Research.* 54 (2): 143.
[149] Sabri and Geraldine, *ibid.,* 236.

[150] Flanagin et al., *ibid.,* 14.

[151] Flanagin et al., *ibid.,* 14.

[152] Flanagin et al., *ibid.,* 16.

[153] Flanagin et al., *ibid.* 17.

[154] Sabri and Geraldoine, *ibid.,* 237.

[155] Lachapelle, E., Montpetit, M. and Gauvin, J-P. (2014). Public Perceptions of expert Credibility on Policy Issues: The Role of Expert Framing and Political Worldviews. *The Policy Studies Journal,* 42 (4): 674.

[156] Lachapelle et al., *ibid.,* 674.

[157] Lachapelle et al., *ibid.*, 674.

[158] Lachapelle et al., *ibid.,* 675.

[159] Lachapelle, et al., *ibid.,* 675.

[160] Flanagin et al., *ibid.,* 6.

[161] Lachappele, et al., *ibid.,* 676.

[162] Lachapelle, et al., *ibid.,* 692.

[163] Lachapelle, et al., *ibid.,* 692.

[164] Jim and Phua, 2014, 181.

[165] Grasse, N. J., Heidbreder, B., and Ihrke, D. M. (2014). City managers' Leadership Credibility: Explaining the Variations of Self-Other Assessments'. *Public Administration Quarterly,* 38 (4): 548.

[166] Grasse et al., *ibid.,* 549.

[167] Jensen, M. L., Averbeck, J. M., Zhang, Z., and Wright, K. B. (2013). Credibility of Anonymous Online Product Reviews: A Language Expectancy Perspective. *Journal of Management Information Systems.* 30 (10): 293-323.

[168] Jensen, et al., *ibid.,* 298.

[169] Jensen, et al., *ibid.,* 299.

[170] [Jensen, et al., *ibid.,* 204.

[171] Jesnsen, et al., *ibid.,* 300.

[172] Fogg, B. J., Marshall, J., Laraki, O., Osipovich, A., Varma, C., Fang, N., Paul, J., Rangnekar, A., Shon, J., Swani, P., and Treinen, M. (2001). What Makes Web Sites credible? A Report on a Large Quantitative Study, *CHI*, 3 (1): 61-68.

[173] Kaur, T., and Dubey, R. K. (2014). Employee Reviews on Company Independent sites and its Impact on Organisational Attractiveness: Role of Information Realism, Person – Environment Fit and source Credibility framework. *Business Theory and Practice,* 15 (4): 393.

[174] Nagle, J. E., Brodsky, S. L., and Weeter, K. (2014). Gender, Smiling, and Witness Credibility in Actual Trials. *Behavioral Sciences and the Law.* 32 (2): 195.

[175] Nagle, Brodsky and Weeter, *ibid.,* 197.

[176] Nagle, Brodsky and Weeter, *ibid.,* 198.

[177] Hur, W-M., Kim, H., and Woo, J. (2014). How CSR Leads to Corporate Brand Equity: Mediating Mechanisms of Corporate Brand Credibility and Reputation. *Journal of Business Ethics.* 125 (1): 75-86.

[178] Smith, A. (1904/1976) *An Inquiry Into the Nature and Causes of The Wealth of Nations*. Chicago: The University of Chicago Press.

[179] Hur, Kim and Woo, *ibid.,* 78.

[180] Myrden, S., and Kelloway, K. (2014). Service Guarantees: The Impact of Playing 'Hard to Get' on Perceptions of Firm Credibility and Repurchase Intent. *Journal of Consumer Satisfaction, Dissatisfaction and Complaining Behavior*, 27: 55 – 69.

[181] Hur, Kim and Woo, *ibid.,* 79.

[182] Olson, *ibid.* 16.

[183] Olson, *ibid.*

[184] Doorley and Garcia, *ibid.*

[185] Doorley and Garcia, *ibid.*

[186] Doorley and Garcia, *ibid.*

[187] Doorley and Garcia, *ibid.*

[188] Doorley and Garcia, *ibid.*

[189] Nelson, B. (2003, February 1). Put their names in lights. In *Meetings Net.* Retrieved from: http://meetingsnet.com/corporate-meetings/put-their-names-lights 13.

[190] Nelson, *ibid.,* 13.

[191] Li, N., Harris, T. B., Zheng, X., and Liu, X. (2016). Recognizing 'Me' Benefits 'We': Investigating the positive Spillover Effects of

Formal Individual Recognition in Teams. *Journal of Applied Psychology* 101 (7): 925.
[192] Li et al., *ibid.,* 925.
[193] Li et al., *ibid.,* 925.
[194] Li et al., *ibid.,* 925-926.
[195] Li et al., *ibid.,* 926.
[196] Castleman, T. (2016). The role of human recognition in development. *Oxford Development Studies,* 44:2, 135-151, DOI: 10.1080/ 13600818.2015.1109615: 139.
[197] Li et al., *ibid.,* 927.
[198] Li et al., *ibid.,* 927.
[199] Li et al., *ibid.,* 927.
[200] Coleman, A. (2010). Local Heroes. *Employee Benefits.* 31.
[201] Coleman, *ibid.,* 32.
[202] Ross and Carter, *ibid.,* 2.
[203] Castleman, *ibid.,* 142.
[204] Castleman, *ibid.,* 143.
[205] Castelman, *ibid.,* 143.
[206] Castleman, *ibid.,* 144.
[207] Fassauer, G. and Hartz, R. (2016). Stories of Adoration and Agony: The Entanglement of Struggles for recognition, Emotions and Institutional Work. *Schmalenbach Business Review* 17:178.
[208] Fassauer and Hartz, *ibid.*, 178.
[209] Fassauer and Hartz, *ibid.,* 178.
[210] Fassauer and Hartz, *ibid.,* 190.
[211] Fassauer and Hartz, *ibid.,* 190.
[212] Castleman, *ibid.,* 145.
[213] Honneth, A. (1996). *The Struggle for Recognition: The Moral of Social Conflicts.* Translated by Joel Anderson. Cambridge, Massachusetts: The MIT Press.
[214] Fassauer and Hartz, *ibid.,* 173.
[215] Sandberg, F and Kubiak, C. (2013). Recognition of prior learning, self-realisation and identity within Axel Honneth's theory of recognition. *Studies in Continuing Education,* 35 (3): 357.

[216] Sandberg and Kubiak, *ibid.,* 357.

[217] Ledingham, J. A. and Bruning, S. D. (1998). Relationship Management in Public Relations: Dimensions of an Organization Public Relationship. *Public Relations Review* 24 (1): 55.

[218] Ledingham and Brunig, *ibid.,* 56.

[219] Ledingham and Brunig, *ibid.,* 56.

[220] Brunner, B. R. (2008). Listening, Communication and Trust: Practitioners' Perspectives of Business/Organizational Relationships. *International Journal of Listening, 22*(1), 73-82.

[221] Gombita, J. (2011, November 14). Connections Byte: Chewing on relationship Building in PR vis. Social Media. Retrieved from: www.business2community.com/public-relations/connections-byte-chewing-on-relationship-building-in-pr-vs-social-media-087326#ez5vYXbyUlmcm161.97.

[222] Boie, C. (2012). Public Relations and Relationship Management Theory. Institutional Perspectives. *Revista Transilvanä de Ştinte ale Comunicäri,* 1 (15): 3-18.

[223] Childers Hon, L. and Grunig, J. E. (1999). Guidelines for Measuring relationships in Public Relations. *Institute for Public Relations.* Retrieved from: www.instituteforpr.org. 2.

[224] Childers and Grunig, *ibid.,* 2.

[225] Childers and Grunig, *ibid.,* 2.

[226] Childers and Grunig, *ibid.,* 7.

[227] Doorley and Gracia, *ibid.,* 73.

[228] Doorley and Gracia, *ibid.,* 18.

[229] Doorley and Gracia, *ibid.,* 21.

[230] Bowen, S. (2007). Ethics and Public Relations. IPR – Institute for Relations. 9.

[231] Bruhn, J. G., Zajac, G., Al-Kazemi, A. A., Prescott, L. D. Jr. (2002). 'Moral Positions and Academic Conduct: Parameters of Tolerance for Ethics Failure,' *The Journal of Higher Education,* 73 (4): 477.

[232] Bruhn et al., *ibid.,* 28.

[233] Argyris, C. (1985). *Strategy, Change and Defensive Routines.* Boston, MA: Pitman.

[234] Bruhn, J. G. (2008). 'Value Dissonance and Ethics Failure in Academia: A Casual Connection?' *Journal of Academic Ethics,* 6: 28.

[235] Bruhn, *ibid.,* 29.

[236] Bruhn, *ibid.,* 29.

[237] Bruhn, *ibid.,* 29.

[238] Bruhn, *ibid.,* 30.

[239] Gower, K. K.. 2006. Public Relations Research at the Crossroads, *Journal of Public Relations Research,* 18 (2): 177-190.

[240] Gower, *ibid.*

[241] Mersham, et al., *ibid.*

[242] Kirby, S. (2007). 'The evolution of language,' in Dubar and Barrett (eds.), *Oxford Handbook of Evolutionary Psychology*, 669-681.

[243] Thomas, M. W. (2003). 'Textual Archaeology: Lessons in the history of business writing pedagogy from a medieval Oxford scholar', *Business Communication Quarterly,* 66 (3): 99.

[244] Wolff, L. M. (1979). A Brief History of the Art of Dictamen: Medieval Origins of Business letter writing. *The Journal of Business Communication*. 16: 2. 5.

[245] Wolff, *ibid.,* 5.

[246] Wolff, *ibid.,* 5.

[247] Wolff, *ibid.,* 5.

[248] Thomas, *ibid.,* 100.

[249] Thomas, *ibid.,* 100.

[250] Carbone, *ibid.,* 175.

[251] Grice, H. P. (1989). *Studies in the Way of Words*, Cambridge, MA: Harvard University Press.

[252] Rorty, R. (1989). *Contingency, Irony and Solidarity,* Cambridge: Cambridge Press: 113.

[253] Grice, H. P. (1989). *Studies in the Way of Words*. Harvard: Harvard University Press 44.

[254] Grice, *ibid.,* 44.

[255] Grice, *ibid.,* 31.

[256] James, N. (2007). *Writing at Work. How to write clearly, effectively and professionally*. Crows Nest NSW, Australia: Allen and Unwin. 39.

[257] James, *ibid.,* 40.

[258] James, *ibid.,* 40.

[259] James, *ibid.,* 41.

[260] James, *ibid.,* 252.

[261] James, *ibid.,* 245.

[262] Ebel, H. F., Bliefert, C., and William E. Russey. (2004). 'The Art of Scientific Writing.' In *From Student Reports to Professional Publications in Chemistry and Related Fields.* Weinheim, FRG: Wiley: 3.

[263] Ebel et al.*, ibid.,* 3.

[264] Ebel et al., *ibid.,* 3.

[265] Bivins, T. H. (2008). *Public Relations writing: The Essentials of Style and Format.* (7th edit). New York: McGraw-Hill: 2.

[266] Bivins, *ibid.,* 5.

[267] Bivins, *ibid.,* 9.

[268] Bivins, *ibid.,* 10-11.

[269] Bivins, *ibid.,* 11.

[270] Bivins, *ibid.,* 13.

[271] Bivins, *ibid.* 10-11.

[272] Bivins, *ibid.,* 48.

[273] Bivins, *ibid.,* 49-50.

[274] Petty, R. E., Cacioppo, J. T., Schumann, D. (1983). Central and Peripheral Routes to Advertising Effectiveness: The Moderating Role of Involvement. *Journal of Consumer Research*. Vol. 10: 135-146.

[275] Carbone, M. T. (1994). The History and Development of Business Communication Principles: 1776-1916. *The Journal of Business Communication.* 31: 3, 179.

[276] Bivins, *ibid.,* 47.

[277] Bivins, *ibid.,* 51.

[278] Bivins, *ibid.,* 151.

[279] Bivins, *ibid.,* 68.

[280] Carbone, *ibid.,* 173.

[281] Smith, J. (2012). The company with the best CSR reputations. Forbes. Retrieved from: http://www.forbes.com/sites/jacquelynsmith/2012/12/10/the-companies-with-the-best-csr-reputations/208.

[282] Doorley and Garcia, *ibid.,* 275.

[283] Smith, *ibid.,*209.

[284] Smith, *ibid.,* 212.

[285] Smith, *ibid.,* 213.

[286] Smith, *ibid.,* 218.

[287] Mersham, et al*., ibid.* 113.

[288] Doorley and Garcia, *ibid.,* 274.

[289] Coombs, T. (2007). *Institute For Public Relations.* Retrieved from: http://www.instituteforpr.org/crisis-management-and-communications/.

[290] Coombs, *ibid.*

[291] Coombs, *ibid.*

[292] Coombs, *ibid.*

[293] Coombs, *ibid.*

[294] Coombs, *ibid.*

[295] Mersham, et al*., ibid.*

[296] Mersham, et al*., ibid.*

[297] Mersham, et al*., ibid. 113.*

[298] Garg, P., Rastog, R. and Kataria, A. (2013) The influence of organisational justice on organizational citizenship behaviour. *International Journal of Business and Management* 6 (2): 84.

[299] Doorley, and Garcia, *ibid.,* 346.

[300] Garg, et al*., ibid,* 84.

[301] Garg, et al*., ibid.,* 84.

[302] Inglis, D. (2012). Aletrnative histories of cosmopolitanism. Reconfiguring classical legacies. In G. Delanty, (Ed.), *Routledge Handbook of Cosmopolitan Studies.* New York; Routledge, 15.

[303] Huntington, S. P. (1993). 'The Clash of Civilizations?' *Foreign Affairs,* 72 (3): 25.

[304] Garg, *ibid.,* 84.

[305] Garg, *ibid.,* 85.

[306] Hoy and Tarter, C. J. (2004). Organizational Justice in Schools: No Justice Without Trust. *International Journal of Educational Management,* 18 (4).

[307] Rapport, N. (2012). Emancipatory Cosmopolitanism. A Vision of The Individual Free from Culture, Custom and Community. In G. Delanty (Ed.). *Routledge Handbook of Cosmopolitan Studies.* New York: Routledge: 102.

[308] Bateman, T. S., and Organ, D. W. (1983). Job satisfaction and the good soldier: The relationship between affect and employee 'citizenship'. *Academy of Management Journal*, 26 (4).

[309] Garg, et al*., ibid.,* 84.

[310] Garg, et al*., ibid.,* 88.

[311] Garg, et al*., ibid.,* 88.

[312] Sison, A. J. G. (2011). Aristoelian citizenship and corporate citizenship: Who is a citizen of the corporate polis? *Journal of Business Ethics,* 100, 3.

[313] Sison, *ibid.,* 8.

[314] Sison, *ibid.,* 4.

[315] Sison, *ibid.* 3.

[316] Moon et al*., ibid.,* 440.

[317] Sison, *ibid.,* 7.

[318] Sison, ibid., 7.

[319] Stokes, G. (2002). Democracy and Citizenship. In April carter and Geoffrey Stokes (Edit.). *Democratic Theory Today.* Stuttgart: Schaffer-Poeschel: 23.

[320] Locke, J. (1689/1988). *Two Treatises of Government.* P. Laslett (Edit.) Cambridge: Cambridge University Press.

[321] Moon et al*., ibid.,* 440.

[322] Moon et al*., ibid,* 442.

[323] Stokes, *ibid.,* 39-44.

[324] Moon, et al*., ibid,* 444.

[325] Moon, et al*., ibid.,* 447.

[326] Klotz, A. C. and Bolino, M. C. (2013) Citizenship and counterproductive work behaviour: A moral licensing view. *Academy of Management Review,* 38 (2): 292.

[327] Klotz and Bolino, *ibid.,* 292.

[328] Klotz and Bolino, *ibid.,* 294.

[329] Knight, C. (2011). In Defence of Cosmopolitanism. *Theoria: A Journal of Social and Political Theory, 58* (129): 19.

[330] Knight, *ibid.,* 19.

[331] Knight, *ibid.,* 20.

[332] Klotz and Bolino, *ibid.,* 292.

[333] Klotz and Bolino, *ibid.,* 292.

[334] Klotz and Bolino, *ibid.,* 264.

[335] Klotz and Bolino, *ibid.,* 294.

[336] Klotz and Bolino, *ibid.,* 297.

[337] Morris, L. (2013) Cosmopolitanisms – beyond the 'beautiful idea'. *Irish Journal of Sociology,* 20 (2): 52.

[338] Morris, *ibid.,* 52.

[339] Morris, *ibid,* 54.

[340] Morris, *ibid.,* 56.

[341] Lockwood, D. (1996). Civic Integration and Class Formation. *British Journal of Sociology,* 47 (3): 536.

[342] Morris, *ibid.,* 57.

[343] Morris, *ibid.,* 62.

[344] Morris, *ibid.,* 63.

[345] Calloni, M. (2012) Cosmopolitanisms and the Negotiation of Borders. *Irish Journal of Sociology,* 20 (2): 154.

[346] Doorley and Garcia, *ibid.,* 342.

[347] Doorley and Garcia, *ibid.,* 343-344.

[348] Beck, U. (1982). *The Risk Society.* London, England: Sage Publications: 3.

[349] Beck, *ibid.,* 4.

[350] Dowling, G. R. (1994). *What are Corporate Reputations? Corporate Reputations: Strategies Benefits from Brands* (after Keller (2008),

and Kelly and Jurgenheimer (2008)). Melbourne, Australia: Longman Professional: 167.

[351] Fombrun, C. (1996). *Reputation: Realizing Value from the Corporate Image.* Cambridge, MA: Harvard Business School Press: 72.

[352] Dowling, G. R. (2001). *Corporate Reputations: Strategies for Developing Corporate Brand.* Melbourne: Longman Professional. x.

[353] Brown cited in Peet, J. (n.d.) *Sustainability in New Zealand – Lifting the game* [Sustainability review background paper]. Retrieved February 8, 2009, from http://www.pce.govt.nz/_data/assets/pdf_file/0014/1634/sustain.pdf.

[354] Chevallier, C., Molesworth, C., and Happe, F. (2011). Diminished social motivation negatively impacts reputation management: Autism spectrum disorder a case in point. *Plos One7* (1), 1.

[355] Osgood, C.E., Suci, G., and Tannenbaum, P. (1957). *The Measurement of Meaning.* Urbana, IL: University of Illinois Press.

[356] Kong, E. and Farrell, M. (2010). The role of image and reputation as intangible resources in non-profit organisations: A relationship management perspective. In ICICKM 2010: 7th International Conference on Intellectual Capital, Knowledge Management and Organisational Learning, 11–12 Nov 2010, Hong Kong, China.: 246.

[357] Doorley and Garcia, *ibid.,* 339.

[358] Fombrun, *ibid.,* 67.

[359] Sherofsky, F. J. (1997). Does character really affect business? In *Perfecting corporate characters: Insightful lessons for 21stcentury organizations* (pp. 3- 9). Clinton Twp., MI: Strategic Publications. 3.

[360] Fox, C. J., and Miller, H. T. (1995). Postmodern public administration: Toward discourse. Thousand Oaks, CA: Sage. González-Herrero, A. & Pratt, C.B. (1996). An integrated symmetrical model for crisis - communication management. *Journal of Public Relations Research,* 8(2), 10.

[361] Burnier, D. (2005). Making it meaningful: Postmodern public administration and symbolic interactionism. *Administrative Theory and Praxis,* 27 (3), 499.

[362] Burnier, *ibid.,* 502.

[363] Zabala, I., Panadero, G., Gallardo, L. M., Amate, C. M., Sanchez-Galind, O, M., Tena, I, and Villalba, I. (2005). Corporate Reputation in Professional Service Firms: Reputation Management Based on Intellectual Capital Management, *Corporate Reputation Review* 8 (1): 59.

[364] Zabala et al., *ibid.* 59.

[365] González-Herrero, A. and Pratt, C.B. (1996). An integrated symmetrical model for crisis - communication management. *Journal of Public Relations Research,* 8(2), 10.

[366] Lauzen, M. A. (1997). Understanding the relation between Public Relations and issues management. Journal of Public Relations Research, 9(1), 65–82.

[367] Coombs, *ibid.*

[368] Scott, S. V. & Walsham, G. (2005). Reconceptualising and managing reputation risk in the knowledge economy: Toward reputable action. Organization Science, 16(3):308.

[369] Scott and Walsham, *ibid.,* 308.

[370] Scott and Walsham, *ibid.,* 309.

[371] Doorley and Garcia, *ibid,* 4.

[372] Doorley and Garcia, *ibid,* 13.

[373] Beal, D. J., Goyen, M., and Phillips, P. (2005). Why do we invest ethically? *The Journal of Investing,* 14 (3): 66-78.

[374] Russell, J. D. and Brockman, C. M. (2011). Do shareholders benefit from sound corporate citizenship? An empirical investigation of the best corporate citizens. *Review of Business Research,* 11 (5): 21-32.

[375] Zambon, S., and Marzo, G. (2007). *Visualizing Intangibles: Measuring and Reporting in the Knowledge Economy.* Hampshire: Ashgate: 51.

[376] Zambon, S., and Marzo, *ibid.,* 2.

[377] Kay, J. (2004). *The Truth About Markets – Why Some Nations Are Rich but Most Remain Poor*. New York: Harper Collins: 174.

[378] Mersham, G. M., and Sandilands, A. (2009). Reputation, image and identity. In G. M. Mersham, P. Theunissen & J. Peart. (Eds.), *Public relations and communication management: an Aotearoa/ New*

Zealand perspective (pp. 217 - 231). Auckland, New Zealand: Pearson Education: 220.

[379] Andriessen, D. (2003). *Making Sense of intellectual capital designing a Method for the valuation in the Intangible Economy.* Oxford: Elsevier Butterworth Heinemann. 5.

[380] Andriessen, *ibid.,* 5.

[381] Perelman, M. (2006). *The Perverse Economy: Scarcity, Extraction and Value in economic Theory.* New York: Palgrave. Macmillan. 79.

[382] Perelman, *ibid.,* 81.

[383] Perelman, *ibid.,* 82.

[384] Mill, J. S. (1848, 1909) in W. J. Ashley (Edit.). *Principles of Political Economy with some of their Applications to Social Philosophy*. (7th edition). London: Longmans, Green and Co. 456.

[385] Mirowski, P. (1989). *More Heat than Light: Economics as Social Physics, Physics as Nature's Economics.* Cambridge: Cambridge University Press. 271.

[386] Perelman, *ibid.,* 91.

[387] Perelman, *ibid.,* 93.

[388] Perelman, *ibid.,* 97.

[389] Robbins, L. (1935). *An essay on the nature and significance of economic science*. Second Edition). London: MacMillan: 19.

[390] Ho, Y. K., Xu, Z. and Yap, C. M. (2004). 'R&D Investment and Systematic Risk'. *Accounting and Finance,* 44: 393-418.

[391] Wyatt, S. (2002). 'Accounting for Intangibles: The Great Divide Between Obscurity in Innovation Activities and the Balance Sheet', *Singapore Economic Review,* 42 (1): 83-117.

[392] Marzo, G. 'Intangibles and Real options Theory: A Real Measurement Alternative' in Zambon, S. and Giuseppe Marzo. (2007). *Visualizing Intangibles: Measuring and Reporting in the Knowledge Economy.* Hampshire: Ashgate: 36.

[393] Marzo, *ibid.* 49.

[394] Doorley and Gracia, *ibid.,* 12-13.

[395] Doorley and Gracia, *ibid.,* 12-13.

[396] Doorley and Gracia, *ibid.,* 12-13.

[397] Doorley and Gracia, *ibid.,* 12-13.

[398] Williams, M. (2013). North Korea's Internet returns after 36-hour outage. *Computer World.*

[399] Hofilena, J. (2013). Japanese advisor Lijima visits North Korea, no official statement on purpose of visit. *Japan Daily Press.*

[400] Sieg, L. (2013). 'U. S. stresses coordination after Japan PM's aide visits North Korea' Reuters, U. K.

[401] McQuail, D. (1998). *Mass communication theory: An Introduction.* (3rd Edit.). London, England: Sage.

[402] Perlroth, N (2014). North Korea Loses its Link to the Internet. *The New York Times.*

[403] Evans, S. (2014). Why did North Korea's internet go down? *BBC. Asia.*

[404] Signorielli, and Gerbner, (1988) *Violence and Terror in the Mass Media: An Annotated Bibliography.* New York: Greenwood Press 1.

[405] Signorielli, and Gerbner, *ibid.,* 7.

[406] Signorielli, and Gerbner, *ibid.,* 7.

[407] Signorielli, and Gerbner, *ibid.,* 8.

[408] Signorielli, and Gerbner, *ibid.,* 8.

[409] Bernstein, R. (2002) *What is noise? Navigate the Noise: Investing in the New Age of Media and Hype.* Hoboken, NJ: Wiley.9.

[410] Bernstein, *ibid.,* 9.

[411] Bernstein, *ibid.,* 9.

[412] Bernstein, *ibid.,* 9.

[413] Bernstein, *ibid.,* 9.

[414] Boorstin, D. J. (1961) The image: A guide to pseudo-events in America. New York, NY: Vintage: 16.

[415] Boorstin, *ibid.,* 17.

[416] Signorielli, and Gerbner, *ibid.,* 2.

[417] Boorstin, *ibid.,* 18.

[418] Boorstin, *ibid.,* 19.

[419] Boorstin, *ibid.,* 20.

[420] Boorstin, *ibid.,* 19.

[421] García de Madariaga JM (2013) New mediations in the digital age: An analysis of global communication through professional journalists. In K. Wilkins, J. Straubhaar, & S. Kumar (Eds.), *Global Communication: New Agendas in Communication* (pp. 183-200). Hoboken, NJ: Taylor & Francis. 19.

[422] de Madariaga, De, G. *ibid.,* 186.

[423] Boorstin, *ibid.,* 19.

[424] Doorley and Gracia, *ibid.,* 2.

[425] Doorley and Gracia, *ibid.*

[426] Doorley and Garcia, *ibid.,* 39.

[427] Lee, S. (2005). The emergence of global public and international Public Relations. *Public Relations Quarterly*, *50*,(2), 14-16.

[428] Lee, *ibid.* 14.

[429] Guy, J-S. (2009). What is global and what is local? A theoretical discussion around globalization. *The Parsons Journal For Information Mapping*. New York. Retrieved from: http://piim.newschool.edu/journal/issues/2009/02/pdfs/ParsonsJournalForInformationMapping_Gu-JeanSebastian.pdf.

[430] Guy, *ibid.*

[431] Hardt, H. (1979) *Social theories of the press*. Beverly Hills, California: Sage Publications. 35.

[432] Pal, M., & Dutta, M. J. (2008). Public Relations in a global context: The relevance of critical modernism as a theoretical lens. *Journal of Public Relations Research, 20* (2), 161.

[433] Pal and Dutta, *ibid.*

[434] Pal and Dutta, *ibid.*

[435] Li, C., and Bernoff, J. (2008). *Groundswell: Winning in a world transformed by social technologies*. Boston, Massachusetts: Harvard Business Press. 46.

[436] Benkler, Y. (2006). *The Wealth of Networks: How Social Production Transforms Markets and Freedom.* New Haven and London: Yale University Press. 376.

[437] Grieco, M.S. and Hosking, D. M. (1987). Networking, Exchange, and Skill. *International Studies of Management and Organisation.* Xvii (1), 75.

[438] Grieco and Hosking, *ibid.,* 81.

[439] Grieco and Hosking, *ibid.,* 82.

[440] Bianchi, A. (2012) Never Say I! Networking as a disciplinary system: Exit strategies. *Technoetic Arts: A Journal of Speculative Research.* 10 (1), 79.

[441] Bianchi, *ibid.,* 66.

[442] Donde, D.S., Chopped, N., and Ranjith, P. V. (2012). Social Networking Sites - A New Era of 21st Century. *SIES Journal of Management*. 8 (1), 66.

[443] Donde, Chopeed and Ranjith, *ibid.,* 67.

[444] Brown, J. S., and Dugoid, P. (2000). *The Social Life of Information.* Boston, Massachusetts: Harvard Business School: 226.

[445] [Donde, Chopeed and Ranjith, *ibid.,* 67.

[446] Todd, S. Y., Harris, K.J., Harries, R. B., and Wheeler, A. R. (2009). Career success implications of political skill. *The Journal of Social Psychology.* 149 (3), 179.

[447] Todd et al.*, ibid.* 180.

[448] Todd et al.*, ibid.,* 180.

[449] Todd et al.*, ibid.,* 180.

[450] Todd et al.*, ibid.,* 180.

[451] Grieco and Hosking, *ibid.,* 82.

[452] Todd et al.*, ibid.,* 182.

[453] Todd et al.*, ibid.,* 182.

[454] Todd et al.*, ibid.,* 182.

[455] Doorley and Garcia, *ibid.,* 208-209.

[456] Todd et al.*, ibid.,* 183.

[457] Harris, K. J., Kacmar, K. M., Zinuska, S., Shaw, J. D. (2007). The impact of political skill on impression management effectiveness. *Journal of Applied Psychology*, 92 (1): 278-85.

[458] Todd et al.*, ibid.,* 186.

[459] Levy, D. A., Collins, B. E., and Nail, P. R. (1998). A New Model of Interpersonal Influence Characteristics. *Journal of Social Behavior and Personality,* 13 (4): 715-733.

[460] Todd et al., *ibid.,* 186.

[461] Todd et al., *ibid.,* 186.

[462] Todd et al., *ibid.,* 186.

[463] Todd et al., *ibid.,* 185.

[464] Todd et al., *ibid.,* 185.

[465] Todd et al., *ibid.,* 199.

[466] Clipson, T. W. and Wilcon, S. A., and DuFrene, D. D. (2012). The Social Networking Arena: Battle of the Sexes. *Business Communication Quarterly*. 75 (1), 64.

[467] Clipson, Wilcon and DuFrene, *ibid.,* 65.

[468] Comscore, *ibid.* 66.

[469] Clipson, Wilcon and DuFrene, *ibid.,,* 65.

[470] Comscore, *ibid.,* 66.

[471] Semrau, T., and Sigmund, S. (2010). The Impact of Networking Ability on New Venture Performance. *Academy of Management Proceedings*, 1-6, doi: 10.5465/AMBPP.2010.54494959. 1.

[472] Semrau T., and Sigmund, S. *ibid.,* 5.

[473] Norris, E., Alexander, H., Livingston, M., Woods, K., Fischbacher, M., and MacDonald, E. (2005). 'Multidisciplinary perspectives on core networking skills. A study of skills: and associated training needs, for professionals working in managed clinical networks'. *Journal of Interprofessional Care*. 19 (20), 156.

[474] Norris et al., *ibid.,* 156.

[475] Norris et al., *ibid.,* 156.

[476] Shi, J., Chen, Z., and Zhou, L. (2011). Testing Differential Mediation Effects of Sub-dimensions of Political Skills in Linking Proactive Personality to Employee Performance. *Journal of Business Psychology*. 26, 359.

[477] Shi, Chen, and Zhou, *ibid.,* 359.

[478] Shi, Chen, and Zhou, *ibid.,* 359.

[479] Shi, Chen, and Zhou, *ibid.,* 360.

[480] Shi, Chen, and Zhou, *ibid.,* 360.
[481] Shi, Chen, and Zhou, *ibid.,* 360.
[482] Shi, Chen, and Zhou, *ibid.,* 360.
[483] Shi, Chen, and Zhou, *ibid.,,* 360.
[484] Shi, Chen, and Zhou, *ibid.,* 360.
[485] Shi, Chen, and Zhou, *ibid.,* 360.
[486] Shi, Chen, and Zhou, *ibid.,* 361.
[487] Shi, Chen, and Zhou, *ibid.,* 360.
[488] Osberg, T. M., and Raulin, M. L. (1989). Networking as a Tool for Career Advancement among Academic Psychologists. *Teaching of Psychologists.* 16 (1), 26.
[489] Osberg and Maulin, *ibid.,* 26.
[490] Osberg and Maulin, *ibid.,* 26.
[491] Osberg and Maulin, *ibid.,* 27.
[492] Osberg and Maulin, *ibid.,* 27.
[493] Strom, P., and Strom, R. (2012). The Benefits and Limitations of Social Networking. *The Education Digest.* 78 (2), 53.
[494] Zofi, Y. S., and Meltzer, S. (January, 2010). Networking skills to make personal connections. *Long-Term-Living:* 42.
[495] Zofi and Meltzer, *ibid.,*42.
[496] Zofi and Meltzer, *ibid.,* 42.
[497] Zofi and Meltzer, *ibid.,* 42.
[498] Zofi and Meltzer, *ibid.,* 42.
[499] Conole, G., Galley, R., and Culver, J. (2011). Frameworks for understanding the Nature of interactions, Networking, and Community in a Social Networking Site for Academic Practice. *International Review of Research in Open and Distance Learning.* 12 (3), 122.
[500] Zofi and Meltzer, *ibid.,* 42.
[501] Okoro, E. (2012). Social Networking And Pedagogical Variations: An Integrated Approach For Effective Interpersonal And Group Communications Skills Development. *American Journal of Business Education.* 5 (2), 219.
[502] Okoro, *ibid.,* 219.

[503] Kastenmuller, A., Greitemeyer, T., Aydin, N., Tattersall, A. J., Peus, C., Bussman, P., Fischer, J., Frey, D., and Fischer, P. (2011). Terrorism threat and networking: Evidence that terrorism salience decreases occupational networking. *Journal of Organizational Behaviour*. 32, 962.

[504] Dyrud, M. A. (2011). Social Networking and Business Communication Pedagogy: Plugging into the *Facebook* Generation. *Business Communication Quarterly*. 74 (4), 475.

[505] Dyrud, *ibid.,* 476.

[506] Hosting facts. (2017). *Internet Stats & Facts for 2016.* Retrieved from: https://hostingfacts.com/internet-facts-stats-2016/.

[507] Berners-Lee, T., and Fischetti, M. (1999). *Weaving the Web: The Original Design and Ultimate Destiny of the World Wide Web by its inventor.* Britain: Orion Business.

ABOUT THE AUTHOR

Dr. Luke Strongman
Senior Lecturer, Communication
Open Polytechnic

Luke Strongman teaches Communication at the Open Polytechnic in New Zealand. He has published several books.

INDEX

A

B

C

D

E

F

R

S

T

U

V

W